Mometrix
TEST PREPARATION

STAAR

Test Prep Guide Grade 5 Reading Language Arts

I0802507

DEAR FUTURE EXAM SUCCESS STORY

First of all, **THANK YOU** for purchasing Mometrix study materials!

Second, congratulations! You are one of the few determined test-takers who are committed to doing whatever it takes to excel on your exam. **You have come to the right place.** We developed these study materials with one goal in mind: to deliver you the information you need in a format that's concise and easy to use.

In addition to optimizing your guide for the content of the test, we've outlined our recommended steps for breaking down the preparation process into small, attainable goals so you can make sure you stay on track.

We've also analyzed the entire test-taking process, identifying the most common pitfalls and showing how you can overcome them and be ready for any curveball the test throws you.

Standardized testing is one of the biggest obstacles on your road to success, which only increases the importance of doing well in the high-pressure, high-stakes environment of test day. Your results on this test could have a significant impact on your future, and this guide provides the information and practical advice to help you achieve your full potential on test day.

Your success is our success

We would love to hear from you! If you would like to share the story of your exam success or if you have any questions or comments in regard to our products, please contact us at **800-673-8175** or **support@mometrix.com**.

Thanks again for your business and we wish you continued success!

Sincerely,
The Mometrix Test Preparation Team

Written and edited by the Mometrix Exam Secrets Test Prep Team
Printed in the United States of America

Table of Contents

Introduction

Thank you for purchasing this resource! You have made the choice to prepare yourself for a test that could have a huge impact on your future, and this guide is designed to help you be fully ready for test day. Obviously, it's important to have a solid understanding of the test material, but you also need to be prepared for the unique environment and stressors of the test, so that you can perform to the best of your abilities.

For this purpose, the first section that appears in this guide is the **Success Strategies**. We've devoted countless hours to meticulously researching what works and what doesn't, and we've boiled down our findings to the four most impactful steps you can take to improve your performance on the test. We start at the beginning with study planning and move through the preparation process, all the way to the testing strategies that will help you get the most out of what you know when you're finally sitting in front of the test.

We recommend that you start preparing for your test as far in advance as possible. However, if you've bought this guide as a last-minute study resource and only have a few days before your test, we recommend that you skip over the first two Success Strategies since they address a long-term study plan.

If you struggle with **test anxiety**, we strongly encourage you to check out our recommendations for how you can overcome it. Test anxiety is a formidable foe, but it can be beaten, and we want to make sure you have the tools you need to defeat it.

Strategy #1 – Plan Big, Study Small

There's a lot riding on your performance. If you want to ace this test, you're going to need to keep your skills sharp and the material fresh in your mind. You need a plan that lets you review everything you need to know while still fitting in your schedule. We'll break this strategy down into three categories.

Information Organization

Start with the information you already have: the official test outline. From this, you can make a complete list of all the concepts you need to cover before the test. Organize these concepts into groups that can be studied together, and create a list of any related vocabulary you need to learn so you can brush up on any difficult terms. You'll want to keep this vocabulary list handy once you actually start studying since you may need to add to it along the way.

Time Management

Once you have your set of study concepts, decide how to spread them out over the time you have left before the test. Break your study plan into small, clear goals so you have a manageable task for each day and know exactly what you're doing. Then just focus on one small step at a time. When you manage your time this way, you don't need to spend hours at a time studying. Studying a small block of content for a short period each day helps you retain information better and avoid stressing over how much you have left to do. You can relax knowing that you have a plan to cover everything in time. In order for this strategy to be effective though, you have to start studying early and stick to your schedule. Avoid the exhaustion and futility that comes from last-minute cramming!

Study Environment

The environment you study in has a big impact on your learning. Studying in a coffee shop, while probably more enjoyable, is not likely to be as fruitful as studying in a quiet room. It's important to keep distractions to a minimum. You're only planning to study for a short block of time, so make the most of it. Don't pause to check your phone or get up to find a snack. It's also important to **avoid multitasking**. Research has consistently shown that multitasking will make your studying dramatically less effective. Your study area should also be comfortable and well-lit so you don't have the distraction of straining your eyes or sitting on an uncomfortable chair.

The time of day you study is also important. You want to be rested and alert. Don't wait until just before bedtime. Study when you'll be most likely to comprehend and remember. Even better, if you know what time of day your test will be, set that time aside for study. That way your brain will be used to working on that subject at that specific time and you'll have a better chance of recalling information.

Finally, it can be helpful to team up with others who are studying for the same test. Your actual studying should be done in as isolated an environment as possible, but the work of organizing the information and setting up the study plan can be divided up. In between study sessions, you can discuss with your teammates the concepts that you're all studying and quiz each other on the details. Just be sure that your teammates are as serious about the test as you are. If you find that your study time is being replaced with social time, you might need to find a new team.

Strategy #2 – Make Your Studying Count

You're devoting a lot of time and effort to preparing for this test, so you want to be absolutely certain it will pay off. This means doing more than just reading the content and hoping you can remember it on test day. It's important to make every minute of study count. There are two main areas you can focus on to make your studying count.

Retention

It doesn't matter how much time you study if you can't remember the material. You need to make sure you are retaining the concepts. To check your retention of the information you're learning, try recalling it at later times with minimal prompting. Try carrying around flashcards and glance at one or two from time to time or ask a friend who's also studying for the test to quiz you.

To enhance your retention, look for ways to put the information into practice so that you can apply it rather than simply recalling it. If you're using the information in practical ways, it will be much easier to remember. Similarly, it helps to solidify a concept in your mind if you're not only reading it to yourself but also explaining it to someone else. Ask a friend to let you teach them about a concept you're a little shaky on (or speak aloud to an imaginary audience if necessary). As you try to summarize, define, give examples, and answer your friend's questions, you'll understand the concepts better and they will stay with you longer. Finally, step back for a big picture view and ask yourself how each piece of information fits with the whole subject. When you link the different concepts together and see them working together as a whole, it's easier to remember the individual components.

Finally, practice showing your work on any multi-step problems, even if you're just studying. Writing out each step you take to solve a problem will help solidify the process in your mind, and you'll be more likely to remember it during the test.

Modality

Modality simply refers to the means or method by which you study. Choosing a study modality that fits your own individual learning style is crucial. No two people learn best in exactly the same way, so it's important to know your strengths and use them to your advantage.

For example, if you learn best by visualization, focus on visualizing a concept in your mind and draw an image or a diagram. Try color-coding your notes, illustrating them, or creating symbols that will trigger your mind to recall a learned concept. If you learn best by hearing or discussing information, find a study partner who learns the same way or read aloud to yourself. Think about how to put the information in your own words. Imagine that you are giving a lecture on the topic and record yourself so you can listen to it later.

For any learning style, flashcards can be helpful. Organize the information so you can take advantage of spare moments to review. Underline key words or phrases. Use different colors for different categories. Mnemonic devices (such as creating a short list in which every item starts with the same letter) can also help with retention. Find what works best for you and use it to store the information in your mind most effectively and easily.

Strategy #3 – Practice the Right Way

Your success on test day depends not only on how many hours you put into preparing, but also on whether you prepared the right way. It's good to check along the way to see if your studying is paying off. One of the most effective ways to do this is by taking practice tests to evaluate your progress. Practice tests are useful because they show exactly where you need to improve. Every time you take a practice test, pay special attention to these three groups of questions:

- The questions you got wrong
- The questions you had to guess on, even if you guessed right
- The questions you found difficult or slow to work through

This will show you exactly what your weak areas are, and where you need to devote more study time. Ask yourself why each of these questions gave you trouble. Was it because you didn't understand the material? Was it because you didn't remember the vocabulary? Do you need more repetitions on this type of question to build speed and confidence? Dig into those questions and figure out how you can strengthen your weak areas as you go back to review the material.

Additionally, many practice tests have a section explaining the answer choices. It can be tempting to read the explanation and think that you now have a good understanding of the concept. However, an explanation likely only covers part of the question's broader context. Even if the explanation makes perfect sense, **go back and investigate** every concept related to the question until you're positive you have a thorough understanding.

As you go along, keep in mind that the practice test is just that: practice. Memorizing these questions and answers will not be very helpful on the actual test because it is unlikely to have any of the same exact questions. If you only know the right answers to the sample questions, you won't be prepared for the real thing. **Study the concepts** until you understand them fully, and then you'll be able to answer any question that shows up on the test.

It's important to wait on the practice tests until you're ready. If you take a test on your first day of study, you may be overwhelmed by the amount of material covered and how much you need to learn. Work up to it gradually.

On test day, you'll need to be prepared for answering questions, managing your time, and using the test-taking strategies you've learned. It's a lot to balance, like a mental marathon that will have a big impact on your future. Like training for a marathon, you'll need to start slowly and work your way up. When test day arrives, you'll be ready.

Start with the strategies you've read in the first two Success Strategies—plan your course and study in the way that works best for you. If you have time, consider using multiple study resources to get different approaches to the same concepts. It can be helpful to see difficult concepts from more than one angle. Then find a good source for practice tests. Many times, the test website will suggest potential study resources or provide sample tests.

Test-Taking Strategies

This section contains a list of test-taking strategies that you may find helpful as you work through the test. By taking what you know and applying logical thought, you can maximize your chances of answering any question correctly!

It is very important to realize that every question is different and every person is different: no single strategy will work on every question, and no single strategy will work for every person. That's why we've included all of them here, so you can try them out and determine which ones work best for different types of questions and which ones work best for you.

Question Strategies

✓ Read Carefully

Read the question and the answer choices carefully. Don't miss the question because you misread the terms. You have plenty of time to read each question thoroughly and make sure you understand what is being asked. Yet a happy medium must be attained, so don't waste too much time. You must read carefully and efficiently.

✓ Contextual Clues

Look for contextual clues. If the question includes a word you are not familiar with, look at the immediate context for some indication of what the word might mean. Contextual clues can often give you all the information you need to decipher the meaning of an unfamiliar word. Even if you can't determine the meaning, you may be able to narrow down the possibilities enough to make a solid guess at the answer to the question.

✓ Prefixes

If you're having trouble with a word in the question or answer choices, try dissecting it. Take advantage of every clue that the word might include. Prefixes can be a huge help. Usually, they allow you to determine a basic meaning. *Pre-* means before, *post-* means after, *pro-* is positive, *de-* is negative. From prefixes, you can get an idea of the general meaning of the word and try to put it into context.

✓ Hedge Words

Watch out for critical hedge words, such as *likely, may, can, often, almost, mostly, usually, generally, rarely,* and *sometimes.* Question writers insert these hedge phrases to cover every possibility. Often an answer choice will be wrong simply because it leaves no room for exception. Be on guard for answer choices that have definitive words such as *exactly* and *always.*

✓ Switchback Words

Stay alert for *switchbacks.* These are the words and phrases frequently used to alert you to shifts in thought. The most common switchback words are *but, although,* and *however.* Others include *nevertheless, on the other hand, even though, while, in spite of, despite,* and *regardless of.* Switchback words are important to catch because they can change the direction of the question or an answer choice.

☑ FACE VALUE

When in doubt, use common sense. Accept the situation in the problem at face value. Don't read too much into it. These problems will not require you to make wild assumptions. If you have to go beyond creativity and warp time or space in order to have an answer choice fit the question, then you should move on and consider the other answer choices. These are normal problems rooted in reality. The applicable relationship or explanation may not be readily apparent, but it is there for you to figure out. Use your common sense to interpret anything that isn't clear.

Answer Choice Strategies

☑ ANSWER SELECTION

The most thorough way to pick an answer choice is to identify and eliminate wrong answers until only one is left, then confirm it is the correct answer. Sometimes an answer choice may immediately seem right, but be careful. The test writers will usually put more than one reasonable answer choice on each question, so take a second to read all of them and make sure that the other choices are not equally obvious. As long as you have time left, it is better to read every answer choice than to pick the first one that looks right without checking the others.

☑ ANSWER CHOICE FAMILIES

An answer choice family consists of two (in rare cases, three) answer choices that are very similar in construction and cannot all be true at the same time. If you see two answer choices that are direct opposites or parallels, one of them is usually the correct answer. For instance, if one answer choice says that quantity *x* increases and another either says that quantity *x* decreases (opposite) or says that quantity *y* increases (parallel), then those answer choices would fall into the same family. An answer choice that doesn't match the construction of the answer choice family is more likely to be incorrect. Most questions will not have answer choice families, but when they do appear, you should be prepared to recognize them.

☑ ELIMINATE ANSWERS

Eliminate answer choices as soon as you realize they are wrong, but make sure you consider all possibilities. If you are eliminating answer choices and realize that the last one you are left with is also wrong, don't panic. Start over and consider each choice again. There may be something you missed the first time that you will realize on the second pass.

☑ AVOID FACT TRAPS

Don't be distracted by an answer choice that is factually true but doesn't answer the question. You are looking for the choice that answers the question. Stay focused on what the question is asking for so you don't accidentally pick an answer that is true but incorrect. Always go back to the question and make sure the answer choice you've selected actually answers the question and is not merely a true statement.

☑ EXTREME STATEMENTS

In general, you should avoid answers that put forth extreme actions as standard practice or proclaim controversial ideas as established fact. An answer choice that states the "process should be used in certain situations, if..." is much more likely to be correct than one that states the "process should be discontinued completely." The first is a calm rational statement and doesn't even make a definitive, uncompromising stance, using a hedge word *if* to provide wiggle room, whereas the second choice is far more extreme.

⊘ BENCHMARK

As you read through the answer choices and you come across one that seems to answer the question well, mentally select that answer choice. This is not your final answer, but it's the one that will help you evaluate the other answer choices. The one that you selected is your benchmark or standard for judging each of the other answer choices. Every other answer choice must be compared to your benchmark. That choice is correct until proven otherwise by another answer choice beating it. If you find a better answer, then that one becomes your new benchmark. Once you've decided that no other choice answers the question as well as your benchmark, you have your final answer.

⊘ PREDICT THE ANSWER

Before you even start looking at the answer choices, it is often best to try to predict the answer. When you come up with the answer on your own, it is easier to avoid distractions and traps because you will know exactly what to look for. The right answer choice is unlikely to be word-for-word what you came up with, but it should be a close match. Even if you are confident that you have the right answer, you should still take the time to read each option before moving on.

General Strategies

⊘ TOUGH QUESTIONS

If you are stumped on a problem or it appears too hard or too difficult, don't waste time. Move on! Remember though, if you can quickly check for obviously incorrect answer choices, your chances of guessing correctly are greatly improved. Before you completely give up, at least try to knock out a couple of possible answers. Eliminate what you can and then guess at the remaining answer choices before moving on.

⊘ CHECK YOUR WORK

Since you will probably not know every term listed and the answer to every question, it is important that you get credit for the ones that you do know. Don't miss any questions through careless mistakes. If at all possible, try to take a second to look back over your answer selection and make sure you've selected the correct answer choice and haven't made a costly careless mistake (such as marking an answer choice that you didn't mean to mark). This quick double check should more than pay for itself in caught mistakes for the time it costs.

⊘ DON'T RUSH

It is very easy to make errors when you are in a hurry. Maintaining a fast pace in answering questions is pointless if it makes you miss questions that you would have gotten right otherwise. Test writers like to include distracting information and wrong answers that seem right. Taking a little extra time to avoid careless mistakes can make all the difference in your test score. Find a pace that allows you to be confident in the answers that you select.

⊘ KEEP MOVING

Panicking will not help you pass the test, so do your best to stay calm and keep moving. Taking deep breaths and going through the answer elimination steps you practiced can help to break through a stress barrier and keep your pace.

Final Notes

The combination of a solid foundation of content knowledge and the confidence that comes from practicing your plan for applying that knowledge is the key to maximizing your performance on test day. As your foundation of content knowledge is built up and strengthened, you'll find that the strategies included in this chapter become more and more effective in helping you quickly sift through the distractions and traps of the test to isolate the correct answer.

Now that you're preparing to move forward into the test content chapters of this book, be sure to keep your goal in mind. As you read, think about how you will be able to apply this information on the test. If you've already seen sample questions for the test and you have an idea of the question format and style, try to come up with questions of your own that you can answer based on what you're reading. This will give you valuable practice applying your knowledge in the same ways you can expect to on test day.

Good luck and good studying!

Reading

Vocabulary

Dictionary

A print or digital dictionary can be used to find out many things about a word. A dictionary will show the correct pronunciation of a word, provide its meaning, and identify what part of speech the word is. It will also tell how the word was derived—that is, what words it came from originally. A dictionary will have a **pronunciation guide** for each word that shows how to sound it out and where its syllables start and end. It will use symbols to indicate sounds, and will also use sample sounds (the "a" in "bad," for instance). A dictionary lists all of the meanings of a word and the parts of speech the word can be used as.

example \ ig-ˈzam-pəl\ noun

1. something that shows what a group of things is like
2. a model that should be either copied or avoided
3. a punishment meant to serve as a warning to others

Example:

Julia used her dictionary to check the various meanings of the word *clear*. She found this entry:

clear (klîr) adjective

1. obvious.
2. easily seen through
3. free from flaw or blemish
4. free from guilt; untroubled
5. out of the way
6. to tidy *v*
7. to free *v*
8. to earn *v*

Identify which definition of *clear* is used in the following sentence:

> Janet stood *clear* of the crowd pushing to get through the door.

The correct answer is meaning 5: "out of the way." If you substitute that definition for the word, the sentence makes sense. Meanings 1, 2, 3, and 4 do not fit with the context of the sentence. Meanings 6, 7, and 8 are verbs and "clear" as it is used in the sample is an adjective. When considering which meaning is being used, always check for context clues in the sentence or in the sentences before or after the sentence in which the word is used.

Thesaurus

A thesaurus is a reference book that gives **synonyms** of words. It is different from a dictionary because a thesaurus does not give definitions. A thesaurus can be helpful in finding the meaning of an unfamiliar word when reading. If the meaning of a synonym is known, then the meaning of the unfamiliar word will be known. Another time in which a thesaurus can be helpful is when writing. Using a thesaurus helps authors to vary their word choice.

Glossary

A glossary is a **list of terms and their definitions** that can be found **at the back** of certain types of books, such as textbooks or reference books. A glossary does not have the definitions of all words, like a dictionary, but instead gives the definitions of the important terms within that particular book which are either uncommon or newly introduced. One may use a glossary when reading a book about economics or a chapter in a science textbook, for example, to define some of the technical terms within the text.

Using Context to Determine the Meanings of Words

Readers of all levels will encounter words that they have either never seen or that they have seen before but still don't know what it means. The best way to define a word in **context** is to look for nearby words that can assist in learning the meaning of the word.

Context Clues

Context clues are hints about the meaning of a word. They are the words or phrases in the sentence or sentences before and after a new or unfamiliar word. Context clues give the reader an idea about what a word means. A context clue may also contain words that help define the new word or an example of what the new word means. Using context clues to figure out meaning can be helpful when learning a new set of vocabulary words or reading a difficult text. The dictionary definition of a word can always be looked up to double-check intended meaning.

Substitution to Find Meaning

One way to find out if you have figured out the correct meaning of a new word is to **substitute** the meaning for the word. Using the example for *reluctant*, if the reader substituted in "not willing," the sentence would read

> Sam was "not willing" to be in the play, so he told the director that he was too busy to rehearse and didn't go to tryouts. He felt to shy to get up on a stage.

Example

Using context clues, determine the meaning of the word *staggered* in the following sentence:

> As soon as he heard his Father's voice, he jumped up from his seat to open the door, but, as he did so, he *staggered* and fell headlong to the floor.

In the example, the word *staggered* refers to the action the character was taking before he "fell headlong to the floor". The reader knows that the character was on his feet, but that he did not have his balance. This information helps the reader decide that the word *staggered* means to move unsteadily.

Synonyms and Antonyms

When you understand how words relate to each other, you will discover more in a passage. This is explained by understanding **synonyms**, which are words that mean the same thing, and **antonyms**, which are words that mean the opposite of one another. As an example, *dry* and *arid* are synonyms, and *dry* and *wet* are antonyms.

Review Video: What are Synonyms and Antonyms?
Visit mometrix.com/academy and enter code: 105612

Example

Read the following sentences and determine the meaning of the word *reluctant* based on context clues:

> Sam was *reluctant* to be in the play, so he told the director that he was too busy to rehearse and didn't go to tryouts. He felt too shy to get up on a stage.

In this example sentence, the words "too busy" show that Sam made an excuse about why he couldn't be in the school play. The sentence also says that he "didn't go to tryouts." The second example sentence has other clues. It says, "He felt too shy to get up on stage." These clues give the reader hints about what the word *reluctant* means. It means "not willing."

Multiple-Meaning Words

A multiple-meaning word has different definitions, depending on the contextual use of the word. A multiple-meaning word is also called a **homonym**. A homonym is defined as a word that has more than one meaning, but is spelled and pronounced the same for all of them. For example, look at the word *leaves* in the following two sentences:

- Michelle *leaves* the building at 5 o'clock every day.
- The *leaves* fell off the oak tree in September.

In the first sentence, *leaves* means exits. In the second sentence, *leaves* refers to parts of a tree. By looking at the rest of each sentence, the reader can understand which definition of the multiple-meaning word the author is referring to.

Similar Words

Homophones are words that are pronounced the same, but may be spelled differently. An example of two homophones would be *heir* (someone due to inherit an estate) and *air* (the invisible substance people breathe).

Homographs are words that are spelled the same, but may be pronounced differently. An example of a homograph is the word *row*, which is pronounced one way when used to mean a horizontal grouping and is pronounced another way when used to mean an argument.

Root Words, Prefixes, and Suffixes

A **root word** is the base word, before an affix, in the form of a prefix, infix, or suffix, is added onto it. Many affixes in the English language come from Latin or Greek origins. A **prefix** is added onto the beginning of a root word, an **infix** is added into the middle, and a **suffix** is added onto the end of a root word. By looking at the meaning of a root word and the meaning of any affixes added to it, the reader can figure out the approximate meaning of the word. For example, the root word 'like' means to enjoy and the prefix 'dis-' means not. The reader can therefore understand that the full word 'dislike' means to not enjoy.

A reader can use root words and affixes to figure out the general meaning of an unknown word. Knowing root words and affixes is helpful on tests where analogies are made using unfamiliar words. By figuring out the general meaning of a new word, a tester can figure out the general relationship presented between two words.

Common Greek Root Words

Root	Meaning	Example
auto	self	automobile (a self-propelled vehicle)
geo	earth or ground	geography (study of the earth)
photo	light	photon (a small particle of light)

Common Prefixes

Prefix	Meaning	Example
trans-	across, through, or change	translate (to write or say in a different language)
super-	over or greater than	superhuman (greater than a regular human)
sub-	under	submerge (to sink below the surface)

Common Suffixes

Suffix	Meaning	Example
-ive	cause to, tend to, or doing	creative (a person who tends to make new things or think of new ideas)
-logy	study of	biology (study of life)
-ful	full of	wonderful (full of wonder)

Example

Using knowledge of affixes, determine meaning of the word *attentive* in the following sentence

> Jorge was a very *attentive* student in Social Studies class, but in Math, he often lost focus.

The word *attentive* contains the suffix "-ive," which means cause to, tend to, or doing. Readers may recognize the beginning of the word, "attent" as the same beginning as the word "attention." Based on the context, the reader can infer that this word means Jorge tends to pay attention in class, especially because of the contrast shown by the second half of the sentence.

Adages

Adages are sayings that describe something that is generally true. For example, "actions speak louder than words" is an **adage**. This adage means that a person's actions show their character more than their words do. Sometimes, adages use figurative language to communicate their true meanings. For example, the saying "the early bird gets the worm" is another adage. This saying means that those who take an opportunity as soon as they can, instead of waiting until later, will be rewarded. Even though the saying's meaning has nothing to do with birds or worms, the saying uses this image to help the recipient understand its real meaning.

Puns

A pun is a phrase that uses a word in an unusual way. **Puns** are usually used to entertain. An example of a pun is found in this excerpt from Lewis Carroll's *Alice's Adventures in Wonderland*:

> *'Mine is a long and a sad tale!' said the Mouse, turning to Alice, and sighing. 'It is a long tail, certainly,' said Alice, looking down with wonder at the Mouse's tail; 'but why do you call it sad?' And she kept on puzzling about it while the Mouse was speaking.*

The author creates a pun using the words "tail" and "tale." In the story, this confuses Alice, but it is meant to entertain the reader.

Chapter Quiz

1. A thesaurus can do all of the following, EXCEPT:

a. Give synonyms of words
b. Give word definitions
c. Help find the meaning of an unfamiliar word
d. Help authors vary their word choice when writing

2. Which of the following are words that sound alike, but are spelled differently and have different meanings?

a. Synonyms
b. Antonyms
c. Homophones
d. Homographs

3. Which of the following is a saying that describes something that is generally true?

a. Adage
b. Pun
c. Analogy
d. Idiom

Chapter Quiz Answer Key

1. B: See section **Thesaurus**

2. C: See section **Similar Words**

3. A: See section **Adages**

Comprehension Skills

Generating Questions About Texts Before, During, and After Reading

Asking questions during the process of reading is one way for you to become a more **active reader**. Active readers do not just sit back and have the content handed to them. Instead, they get involved with the text and are part of the process of learning. Asking questions before you read, pausing to ask questions while you're reading, and asking questions after you read are all good ways to help you become a more active reader. There are three types of questioning that can use as you try to think of questions.

Questioning Yourself

These are questions you ask yourself to see how well you're paying attention, and how involved you are in the story. Some example questions are

- Which character is my favorite so far?
- What do I think is going to happen next?
- Is there a character I am similar to in this story? Do I like those similarities?
- What would I do if I was in this situation?

Questioning the Author

Although the chances are slim that you will ever get the chance to meet most of the authors of the texts you read, another way to get involved in the text is to imagine that you are asking questions of the author him or herself. Some example questions are

- What did the author want me to see here?
- Why did he write about this subject?
- Why did the author use this phrase?
- What did she want the character to learn from this?

Questioning the Text

The last type of question you can ask to improve your reading is called questioning the text. To ask these questions, imagine that you are asking the text itself questions about how it works and what it means. Some examples are:

- What does this word mean?
- What is this paragraph describing?
- Why is this term used here?
- How does this sentence connect to the other sentences in this paragraph?

Predicting What Will Happen in a Story

When you read a story, you should look for clues to make a prediction about what will happen. At the end of the story, you may even think about what will happen next to the main character, and use the clues in the story to make a prediction. You can also use personal experience to help make a prediction.

Suppose there is a story about a boy going swimming, and he swims too far out. Suppose the story says the boy can't get back to shore and starts to yell. Suppose the lifeguard comes and helps him. Suppose the story stops after the boy goes back in the water again. The reader might make the prediction that the boy won't swim as far out this time. This may not be true, but it is the most likely thing to happen.

Example

Describe what prediction can be made based on the following sentences:

> When Glen is sick, his mother keeps him home from school. He stays in bed all day and takes medicine. Glen woke up this morning with a sore throat. His head was hot, and he felt achy.

The story says that Glen's mother keeps him home when he is sick and that Glen spends the day in bed when he is sick. The story says that Glen woke up this morning with a sore throat. His head was hot, and he felt achy. The reader can figure out that Glen was sick. Because Glen's mother always keeps him home when he is sick, the reader can predict that Glen will be staying home from school and spending the day in bed.

You can also use text features find information to make predictions and verify conclusions determined about different texts. Using key words as clues, looking for bold print words, looking for sentences that include captions, and words that are written in italics are a few features that can be used to help understand and make predictions about a text.

Using Structure and Genre to Make Predictions

The structure and genre of a story can also help readers make predictions. Most stories follow the same structure. They have an exposition, rising action, a climax, falling action, and a resolution. Because most stories follow this structure, readers can predict that each of these parts will occur in the story. For example, rising action usually begins after the conflict of the story is introduced. This means that if characters have not faced any conflict, the reader can predict that something will go wrong for the characters. Likewise, stories in the same genre may contain similar events. For example, in a mystery, the characters work to solve a crime or explain a strange event. So, when reading a mystery, the reader can predict that the conflict will be a crime or event that the characters must learn more about.

Making Connections to Enhance Comprehension

Reading involves thinking. For good comprehension, readers make text-to-self, text-to-text, and text-to-world connections. Making connections helps readers understand text better and predict what might occur next based on what they already know, such as how characters in the story feel or what happened in another text. Readers can make connections before, during, and after reading. Venn diagrams and other graphic organizers can help readers visualize connections.

Text-to-Self

Reading while looking for connections with the reader's life and experiences makes literature more personally relevant and meaningful to readers. Sentences showing text-to-self connections may begin with these examples

- This reminds me of a time when...
- I understand how the character feels because...
- The setting makes me think of...
- I experienced this same thing when...

Text-to-Text

Reading while looking for connections to other texts helps the reader learn to identify the way authors use genre, setting, characters, plot elements, literary structure and devices, and themes to create meaning. Sentences showing text-to-text connections may begin with these examples

- The character in this story reminds me of the character in...
- These two stories are alike because...
- The conflict in this story is similar to the conflict in...
- The relationship between the friends in this story is different than the relationship in...

Text-to-World

Reading while looking for connections to the world helps the reader begin to see literature as a reflection of real life and notice patterns in history and current events. Sentences showing text-to-world connections may begin with these examples

- The event in this story sounds like the event in history when...
- The actions of this character sound like...
- This is like what happened in real life when...
- I heard about this on the news when...

Making Inferences

An **inference** is a **conclusion** or generalization that the reader makes based on the information provided within a text. Certain facts are included to help a reader come to a specific conclusion.

For example, a story may open with a man trudging through the snow on a cold winter day, dragging a sled behind him. The reader can infer from the setting of the story that the man is wearing heavy winter clothes in order to stay warm. Information is implied based on the setting of a story, which is why setting is an important element of the text. If the same man in the example was trudging down a beach on a hot summer day, dragging a surf board behind him, the reader would assume that the man is not wearing heavy clothes. The reader makes inferences based on their own experiences and the information presented to them in the story.

Readers may come to their own conclusion about a topic, or the author may state a conclusion at the end of a story. When readers are in the middle of a story, they can predict what will happen at the end of it based on the events that have occurred so far and the typical characteristics that have been presented by the author up to that point. A reader needs to consider all of the information that an author has presented, including the main point and supporting points, to make logical conclusions and inferences about the story.

Sometimes interpreting the information in a sentence can be difficult, especially if the reader is unfamiliar with some of the words used in a sentence. Drawing a picture of what is actually happening in the sentence can help, along with looking at the words that the reader does understand in the sentence. By taking a pen or pencil and underlining important information in a sentence, the reader can better understand what the author is trying to say and draw a clearer conclusion from that. Using context clues, or wording in a sentence, is an important way to identify what the author is talking about in the story. An author will often leave blanks for the reader to fill in on their own, using information that has been presented up to that point in the story.

Example

Describe what can be inferred from the following sentences:

> Sometimes after a big storm, the beaches are covered with dead fish, seaweed, broken shells, and pieces of wood. Most seaweed is brown or gold, but there are often pieces of white seaweed. If people visit the beaches, the white seaweed disappears very quickly. It makes a delicious pudding.

To make an inference a reader needs to look for clues in a text. The author does not tell an inference directly; the author hints at one. Here the text says that fish, seaweed, and shells are on the beach after a storm. It also says that some of the seaweed is white and adds that the white seaweed is used for pudding. Another clue is that the white seaweed disappears quickly if people visit the beaches. The inference that a reader can figure out is that the people take the seaweed. It disappears quickly because it can be used to make a delicious pudding.

EXAMPLE

Read the following two sentences and draw a conclusion based on the text:

> Sarah worked hard on her science project. Her presentation of the science project to the class went well.

Based on the two sentences, the reader can conclude that Sarah will receive a high grade on her science project. The reader knows that Sarah put a great deal of time and effort into her project and that the actual presentation of the project was successful. Based on these facts, the reader can assume that the teacher will appreciate and reward Sarah's effort. This conclusion can be drawn based on the reader's knowledge of how high grades are obtained and their own previous experience with school projects. The reader can assume that Sarah's assessment of her presentation is accurate, that the presentation did indeed conform to high expectations. When a conclusion is drawn based on information the reader is given in a text, the conclusion is called an *inference.*

EXAMPLE

Read the following sentence. Draw a conclusion based upon the information presented.

> "A rosy-faced servant-maid opened the door, and smiled as she took the letter which he silently offered."

The reader can conclude, based on the sentence, that the servant-maid is friendly. The words "rosy-faced" and "smiled" lead the reader to this conclusion. People who are friendly are often described as having rosy complexions and smiling as a common sign of pleasantness. The reader can also assume, from the sentence, that the letter does not present any threat or unpleasantness to the servant-maid. The person presenting the letter does not have anything to say upon offering it, so perhaps he is waiting to see how the servant-maid will react.

When interpreting a sentence, always look for key words that describe a character. The author carefully crafts a description of each character, to form a picture in the reader's mind about what the character is like.

KEY IDEAS AND SUPPORTING DETAILS

Identifying **key ideas** helps the reader see what a text or story is mostly about. They are the **most important ideas** in a text, and everything else in the text builds around and supports them. Every piece of writing has key ideas. The **supporting details** in a story, such as the characters, events, and settings, will work together to reveal the key ideas. The details are not key ideas, themselves. They make the key ideas clear and show the reader the author's purpose for writing the text.

SYNTHESIZING A TEXT WITH EXISTING KNOWLEDGE

Synthesizing is similar to summarizing but it takes it one step further. Synthesizing involves taking the main points of a text and comparing it with existing knowledge to create a new idea, perspective, or way of thinking.

EXAMPLE

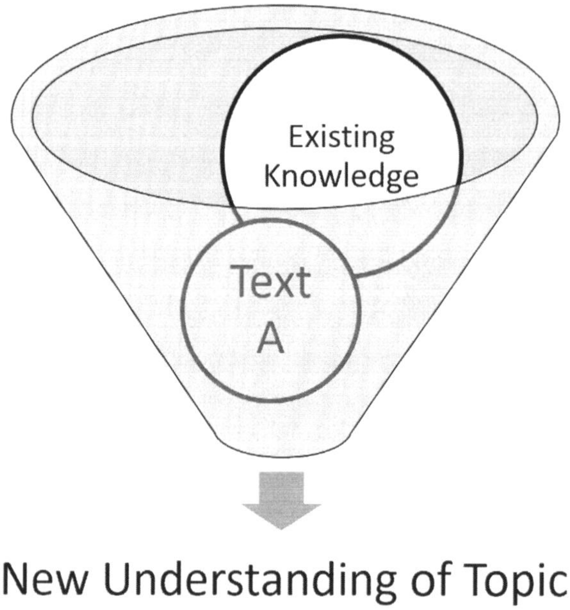

Another term for knowledge that you already have is **schema**. The plural form of this word is **schemata**. Schemata contain all the ideas you have about something. Synthesizing is all about how schemata change over time with the introduction of new information.

Using self-questioning strategies can help readers synthesize texts with their schemata to increase or change their understanding of topics. These questions include

- What do I already know about this topic?
- Is any of this new information?
- Has my perspective changed now that I've read this?
- What do I understand now that I didn't before?
- What are the main ideas of this text?
- How do the parts of the text fit together to create meaning?
- Are there any text-to-text, text-to-self, or text-to-world connections here?

SYNTHESIZING TEXTS WITHOUT EXISTING KNOWLEDGE

If the reader is completely unfamiliar with the topic, they will have no background knowledge. In this case, instead of using existing knowledge, synthesizing may instead be done by combining the ideas provided in two or three different texts. The reader must make connections between the texts, determine how the ideas fit together, and gather evidence to support the new perspective.

CHAPTER QUIZ

1. There are three types of questioning that you can use for active reading. What are these three types of questions?

a. Questioning the composition, grammar, and style of the writing
b. Questioning history, current events, and the future
c. Questioning your personal context, surrounding culture, and the world
d. Questioning yourself, the author, and the text

2. Which of the following helps the reader learn to identify ways authors use genre, setting, characters, plot elements, literary structure and devices, and themes to create meaning?

a. Reading while looking for connections to the reader's life
b. Reading while looking for connections to other texts
c. Reading while looking for connections to the world
d. Reading while looking for connections to history

3. Which of the following is a conclusion that the reader makes using clues in the text?

a. Thesis
b. Prediction
c. Inference
d. Guess

4. What term refers to knowledge that you already have?

a. Cognition
b. Glossary
c. Schema
d. Explicit information

Chapter Quiz Answer Key

1. D: See section **Generating Questions About Texts Before, During, and After Reading**

2. B: See section **Making Connections to Enhance Comprehension**

3. C: See section **Making Inferences**

4. C: See section **Synthesizing a Text with Existing Knowledge**

Response Skills

Text Evidence

The term **text evidence** refers to information found in a text that supports a reader's claim about the text. A reader can draw conclusions or inferences based upon information found in a text. Often, the author will deliberately include information that supports the main point of the text to help the reader make conclusions and inferences that align with the author's purpose for writing the text.

Drawing Conclusions Based on Text Evidence

Readers often need to use prior experience and background information to draw an accurate conclusion about the passage they are reading. Sometimes interpreting the information in a sentence can be difficult, especially if the reader is unfamiliar with some of the words used in a sentence. Looking at the words that the reader does understand in the sentence can help. By taking a pen or pencil and underlining important information in a sentence, the reader can better understand what the author is trying to say and draw a clearer conclusion from that.

Example

Draw a conclusion based on the following quote from *Flora & Ulysses: The Illuminated Adventures* by Kate DiCamillo

> Take this squirrel, for instance. Ulysses. Do I believe he can type poetry? Sure, I do believe it. There is much more beauty in the world if I believe such a thing is possible.

This quote is from the character Dr. Meescham, who is speaking to Flora about her squirrel, Ulysses. Saying a squirrel can type seems silly, but the doctor says he does believe it's true. The phrase "there is much more beauty... if I believe" helps the reader draw the conclusion that Dr. Meescham encourages imagination, and that seeing the world as beautiful is important. The things characters say often show something important about them. Be sure to read dialogue carefully to see what conclusions the author might be wanting you to make.

EXAMPLE

Read the following quote from *Shiloh* by Phyliss Reynolds Naylor and draw a conclusion based upon the information presented.

> Last of all, I take the lard bread from my pocket and feed it to Shiloh in little pieces, letting him lick my fingers after every bite. I wrap my arms around him, pat him, run my hands over his ears, even kiss his nose. I tell him about a million times I love him as much as I love my ma.

The reader can conclude that the narrator adores his dog Shiloh. The words "wrap my arms around him," "kiss his nose," and "tell him about a million times I love him" lead the reader to this conclusion. The reader can also assume that Shiloh loves the narrator as well because he allows all of the touches that he is receiving. Readers know from experience that animals do not often allow touch from people they do not have affection for.

When interpreting a sentence, always look for key phrases that can be used to draw conclusions about characters and their relationships. Authors carefully craft descriptions of each character to form a picture in the reader's mind about what the character is like.

PARAPHRASING AND SUMMARIZING

Paraphrasing and summarizing are two ways readers can work to understand what they read. Both involve reading a text and recalling the main points in an accurate way, but they differ in several ways.

How to Paraphrase	How to Summarize
State the message in the text in the reader's own words, while keeping the original meaning of the text Take all of the original ideas and word them in a way that the reader can better understand Put what the reader has read into their own words, rephrasing what the author has written	State main points of the text clearly and to-the-point. Take information and state it simply, in a much shorter form. Put information in a short form that keeps the main points of the whole text. Do not include many details, just the main idea of the text

Paraphrasing is often done for individual ideas, while summarizing is done for an entire block of text or ideas. Often times, a summary can be done in just one sentence, boiling down the author's words into just main idea.

Review Video: Summarizing Text
Visit mometrix.com/academy and enter code: 172903

PARAPHRASING THE MAIN POINT OF A SENTENCE

Paraphrase the main point of the following two sentences:

> Emmanuel went swimming in the lake by his house, where the water reached a depth of twenty feet in the middle. He did not venture out more than six feet into the water, however.

When paraphrasing a couple sentences or an entire paragraph, always include the main point of the text being reviewed, this is what the reader needs to know about the text. In the example, the reader needs to know that Emmanuel went swimming in the lake, but not more than six feet out. A paraphrase of the text may include: Emmanuel went swimming six feet out in the lake by his house. That is the main point that the audience needs to know.

Recall that a paraphrase is stating the author's ideas in the reader's own words. A summary typically involves including the main points of a longer text, such as a novel or full story.

EXAMPLE

Read the following paragraph and then give a one sentence summary statement:

> When choosing a pet, people need to think about what type of home they can offer the animal. For example, a small apartment might not be a good fit for a large dog, but could be a comfortable home for a kitten. A house that has a big yard would be great for a puppy, but a rabbit does not need a large yard.

In order to summarize, one has to identify the main idea and any supporting ideas in the author's work. The summary is an overview of the author's paragraph and will tell what it is about without getting into any of the details. The summary needs to be broad enough to cover all of the information in the author's paragraph. Here is a possible summary statement for the above paragraph:

> People need to consider a number of factors when choosing a pet.

EXAMPLE

Read the following sentences and then paraphrase the material:

> The government is debating a new health care system for our country. The Senate and the House of Representatives have both passed bills; now they need to resolve these two bills into one bill that a majority can agree on.

When paraphrasing information, one needs to read carefully and pay attention to details, then put the material away and write or tell it in their own words. One does not want to look at the material while paraphrasing to avoid plagiarizing by accident. Here is one example of a way to paraphrase the sentences:

> Our government is trying to adopt a new health care system. The Senate has passed a bill and so has the House of Representatives. Their bills are different so now they have to compromise on one bill that can be passed.

Chapter Quiz

1. If a reader takes an author's original idea and then restates it, putting the idea into their own words, this is an example of:

a. Outlining text
b. Paraphrasing text
c. Summarizing text
d. Abstracting text

2. Which of the following is NOT true of summarizing?

a. A summary can be just one sentence that boils down the author's words into the main idea.
b. Summarizing helps readers work to understand what they have read.
c. A summary typically involves restating the main points of a text in a simpler, shorter fashion.
d. A summary should be subjective and include brief personal opinions on the subject.

Chapter Quiz Answer Key

1. B: See section **Paraphrasing and Summarizing**

2. D: See section **Paraphrasing and Summarizing**

Literary Elements

Theme

The **theme** of a story, essay, or poem is the lesson that it teaches, or the message the author wants to get across. The theme is linked to the characters, the setting, and the events in a story. A passage can have two or more themes that convey its overall idea.

The theme of a story is not the same as the topic of a story. The topic is what the story is about, but the theme is what a reader is meant to learn. When readers are discussing theme, they can determine both theme topics as well as theme statements.

Theme topics are broad ideas that apply to the text. Examples are:

- Love
- The importance of friendship
- Good vs. evil
- The circle of life

Themes may also be complete statements written in sentence form. Examples are:

- Acts of courage can bring positive changes to the world.
- True friendship can withstand the hardest challenges.

Some themes are fairly common. These themes are called **universal themes** and they suggest things about life, society, and human nature.

Themes are very rarely stated in the text. Instead, the reader has to **infer** the theme by reading closely and thinking carefully about what the author is saying.

Themes are an important part of literature because they serve the purpose of teaching the reader or listener a truth about life. The theme is developed by how a character or characters respond to their situations and challenges.

EXAMPLE

Read the following and consider the theme of the excerpt.

> Jeanie arrived at the bake sale early. She bought the biggest cake at the sale. Sally had to work late. When she finally got to the sale, no cakes were left. She got only two cookies. She was lucky to get anything.

The saying "the early bird gets the worm" is one way to explain the theme of the story. In the story we read that Jeanie arrived early at the bake sale and got the biggest cake. But when Sally arrived, all that was left were two cookies. The point of the story is that the early bird gets the worm—the worm in this case is a large cake.

CHARACTERS

CHARACTER TRAIT

The traits of a character may include how they act and physical characteristics; a character trait is a behavior or physical characteristic that is unique to a specific character. For example, a character may be outgoing, which means he or she likes to talk a lot, or they may have bright red hair. These are both character traits.

An author uses character traits to describe a character in a story and help the reader to learn more about how the character acts and what they look like. By comparing the character traits in a story, the reader can see similarities and differences between characters. The author includes character traits to help the reader understand why a character may act a certain way in the story. For example, a character who is shy may not want to talk with a lot of people in a new classroom, but a character who is outgoing may want to talk with many people.

An author typically provides many details about a character so that the reader can learn more about the character's traits, motivations, relationships, and any conflicts they may have in the story. The traits of a character may include how they act and how they look. Characters are often motivated by things that have already happened in their life or how they feel about a topic. The author will often give the reader enough information about the character so that the reader can figure out why the character responds to a situation in a certain way. The author will also often give details about the relationships between characters and points they may conflict on. For example, a character may be good friends with another character; however, the two characters may disagree on where to play outside if one character likes being near the water and the other character does not.

EXAMPLE

Read the following description of a character and decide, logically, whether the character is likely to go hiking outdoors:

> Jeremy lived in a high-rise in Chicago. He was studious, and not very athletic. Jeremy preferred to stay indoors and read a book, rather than enjoy outdoor weather.

Based on the description of the character's traits, preferences, and personality, he is not likely to go hiking outdoors. The description indicates that the character prefers reading, rather than enjoying outdoor weather. In addition, the character lives in a tall building in the middle of a large city, in order for him to enjoy the outdoors, he would have to travel away from where he lives. The character is not likely to change his preferences. A situation may lead the character to go hiking, but he is not likely to initiate the action on his own. A description of a character that is likely to go hiking outdoors may include a preference for outdoor activity and living near trails.

CHARACTER RELATIONSHIPS

A relationship is the way one character acts with another character in a story. The characters are often called **major characters** if they have a main part in the story and **minor characters** if they have a smaller part. There are many different kinds of relationships. For example, two children in a story may be friends, but they could be angry with each other, competing with each other, or helping each other. An author may tell the reader what kind of relationship the characters have. An author might give hints about a relationship. For example, the author may show one child making fun of the other child, which would suggest that the two children do not have a friendly relationship. The author might show one child teaching the other child how to read, which would suggest that the two children have a friendly relationship.

EXAMPLE

Read the following sentences and describe the relationship Jill and Anna have:

> Jill came over to Anna and asked if she wanted an apple. "Sure, I'd love one. Thanks," Anna answered. Anna took a bite of the apple and started to chew it. Her chewing was so loud that they both started to laugh.

The author does not tell what the relationship between Jill and Anna is. The reader must figure it out from their actions. These actions are the clues the author gives. Jill asks Anna if she wants an apple. Anna says yes and starts to eat it. Her chewing is very loud. Both Jill and Anna start to laugh. They seem to like each other. Jill seems generous to Anna because she gives Anna an apple. They laugh together, and friends often laugh together. The reader can use personal experience to decide that it seems as though Jill and Anna are friends.

CHARACTER CHANGES

Characters can change in a multitude of ways throughout a story; however, there are main aspects of a character that change. A character's identifying **characteristics**, such as personality or behavior traits, may change as the result of a prominent event in the story, current **motivations**, and **conflicts**. As conflicts change or are resolved, a character may no longer be motivated by striving toward a goal that was previously important to them. As the plot of a story moves along, characters can constantly change in relation to events that occur. **Relationships** between characters and the points of view of characters may change throughout a story as well.

Each story will have many different types of characters and each of these characters will have a different relationship with other characters. Stories usually have a protagonist, antagonist, and a variety of other characters including round, flat, and stock characters.

PROTAGONIST

The main character in a drama, movie, novel, or other fictional text. The author portrays the protagonist in a way that the audience is most like to identify with themselves. The protagonist is generally undertaking some type of personal challenge throughout the story. The author writes the story so that the reader becomes aware of the protagonist's emotions and is generally able to empathize with the personal challenge.

Antagonist

The character that actively opposes the protagonist by trying to prevent them from succeeding. The antagonist is usually presented in such a way as to make the audience dislike them, and want them to fail at stopping the protagonist. The protagonist and antagonist oppose each other, so their relationship is almost always one of dislike.

Flat Characters

Does not have any substantial changes throughout the story. They stay the same despite the conflict, and do not learn any lessons. They are usually minor characters that might interact with the main character in some way.

Round Characters

Major characters in the story that will be more fully developed than other minor characters. They will usually encounter some type of conflict that they must overcome, and usually learn a lesson about life or themselves along the way.

Stock Characters

Often get their characteristics and mannerisms from stereotypes of people that are widely recognized. These types of characters are often repeated and well-known. Readers should be aware that stereotypes are rarely accurate in reality, and are generally intended to be humorous or dramatic. Some examples are evil stepmothers, unintelligent blondes, rude athletes, and loyal servants.

Plot

The term **plot** refers to the series of events that take place in a story. The events in a story may take place in one location or many, in a short amount of time or over many years. A story always has to start somewhere, and the first event in a story signals the beginning of the plot. Stories may vary in length from half a page to novel-length, but they all follow a progression of events that the author winds together to form the plot. The characters and events in the story determine what the plot will be. Readers may find a **plot line** useful as they try to put the events in the text in order and determine the relationships between events.

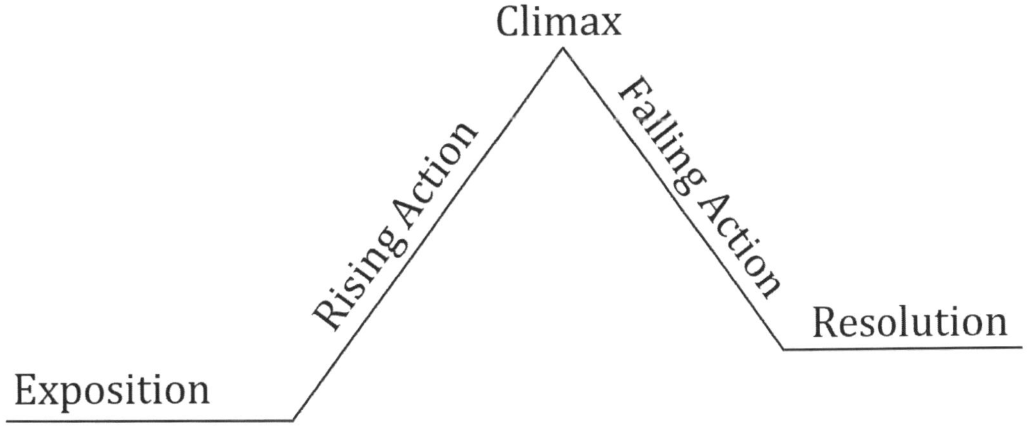

Review Video: Plot Line
Visit mometrix.com/academy and enter code: 944011

Every plot will begin with **exposition**, which introduces the characters and the setting of the story. The plot will continue to develop as new ideas and events centered on the main conflict in the story are revealed, which is called the **rising action**. The action in the story will rise until a **climax** is reached within the conflict. The climax can also be referred to as the turning point in the story, since the climax is where each character makes an important decision. After the climax, the action starts to wind down during the **falling action**. At this point, the characters begin to follow the paths they chose in during climax. The events of the story reach **resolution** in some way by the end of the story. Some conflicts are left open-ended, so that the reader is left to decide what really happened at the end of the story. Keep in mind that not all resolutions are happy or peaceful.

Example

Read the following plot and determine what the missing event is in the plot sequence:

> Sarita went to the store to buy eggs for her mother. She bought the eggs and got back on her bicycle to bring the eggs home. Her mother was angry that the eggs were all broken.

The reader has to guess based on the plot sequence what happened between events. The reader knows that Sarita got on her bicycle to go home. The reader also knows that the eggs were broken when she arrived at the house. Based on the context, the reader can assume that Sarita fell off her bicycle or dropped the eggs on the way home, causing them to all be broken when she arrived. The reader can assume that Sarita would have noticed if the eggs were already broken in the store. Plot often follows a logical sequence of events, but sometimes it is difficult to decide what actually happened between two events. In the example, the reader can logically assume that the eggs were broken on the way home.

Conflict

Conflict creates the basis for the plot of a story. A conflict may be between characters, a character and their own mind, or an outside influence. The main point of a conflict is that there is a problem that needs to be resolved. The problem may be a disagreement or an obstacle that has arisen and needs to be overcome.

An important part of analyzing the plot of a passage is identifying the **main conflict**. There will likely be many smaller conflicts in the story, but there will be one main problem that influences the characters and events. To identify the main conflict, first look at who the main character is. Now ask yourself what they want. They may want to something to happen or not happen, another character to do or not do something, or to confront or avoid a problem, among other things. Once you know what they want, now ask yourself what is standing in the character's way. It may be a person, an event, or something less tangible like the passing of time. Combining what the main character wants and why they do not currently have leaves the reader with a summary of the main conflict.

Review Video: Conflict
Visit mometrix.com/academy and enter code: 559550

Example

Read the following sentence and explain the main conflict between the two characters:

> Joe stared angrily at Jamie's retreating back as Jamie raced away down the field with Joe's soccer ball.

The main conflict in the sentence is that Jamie has Joe's soccer ball. There may be additional conflicts between the two characters, but none are evident from the evidence shown in the sentence. In any story, a conflict may be minor and only affect part of the story, or be the main focus, taking an entire story to solve a conflict between characters. In the context of the sentence, it is not clear whether or not the entire story will revolve around Jamie taking Joe's soccer ball.

Resolution

The term **resolution** usually indicates the result of a conflict in a story. Conflict between characters, within a character, or against an external element is necessary in order to have a plot for a story. Without conflict, no events would occur to form the story. A conflict will come to a climax, and then conclude in some way. The resolution of a problem may be open-ended, end tragically, or end in a way that is good for everyone involved. The problem resolution typically occurs near the end of a story, after the climax has happened. A problem may be resolved by the characters involved within the conflict or by an external event; an upcoming resolution may be foreshadowed in the text, or may be completely unexpected by the reader. If the resolution is completely unexpected, it is considered to be a **twist** in the story.

Effect of Plot on a Story's Characters

The plot of a story unfolds as each event follows another, shaping the characters as they react to the various events that occur. Some characters are able to resolve their problems by the end of the story, while some characters fail to overcome their predicaments. As characters respond to the events around them, they reveal more and more about their personalities. Some grow and some do not. The reader can use the events of the plot to interpret the meaning of the story and understand its characters.

Example

Read the excerpt and explain how finding the chest affects Marta.

> The map said this was the spot. Marta held her breath. Her fists were clenched into two tight balls. She lifted the shovel and scooped more sand out of the hole. There it was; she had found the chest with the diamonds. She opened the top. She would never need to work again. She smiled. It was really happening.

The event affects Marta by making her happy. The reader gets several clues that she is anxiously waiting ("Marta held her breath" and "her fists were clenched"), and that she is happy with what she found ("She smiled"). Events can cause characters to have all kinds of feelings. Here, something wonderful happened. However, events in stories are not always quite so happy. For instance, if a robber had suddenly seen Marta and the chest, he might have stolen the chest. That event would have had a very different effect on her. Readers need to pay attention to how characters are reacting to events, whether they are simply hinted at or stated in the story. In this way a reader will learn what characters are like.

Setting

The setting is where a story **takes place**. The setting of a story may stay the same for the entire story, or change as events in the story unfold. For example, an entire story may take place in one room, or on the other end, a story could cross continents as the reader follows the characters along on a trail of events. Every story has to take place somewhere. The setting of story is described by the author in terms of what it looks like, how the character feels, and anything that is happening at that location at the time. For example, a character may be caught on a doorstep on a cold, rainy day. The character may feel frustrated as he shivers in the doorway, waiting for the heavy rain to let up a bit.

Example

When listing ways that a story set in the city has a different backdrop from a story set in the countryside, answers will vary based on current knowledge of common characteristics for each setting. A story set in a city may be different from a story set in the countryside based on the following factors:

- Number of passersby: many people on a sidewalk vs. no other people around
- Background noise: car horns vs. bird calls
- Types of surroundings: tall buildings vs. fields of corn
- Types of transportation: subways and taxis vs. horses and farm trucks
- Daily activities being carried out: sitting at a desk in a skyscraper vs. plowing fields for planting
- Type of attire: a business suit vs. dirty jeans and boots

Shaping a Character with Setting or Plot

The setting of a story shapes character because it helps to define the situation that a character finds herself in. A character is limited to the setting of a story. For example, if a story takes place in a cold environment filled with snow and ice, this is certain to impact what actions a character can and will take. Frequently, the setting changes the way characters behave based on time. For example, the character of a woman who is a single mother in 1920 would be seen and behave very differently than a single mother in 2020.

Example

Read the excerpt and determine how the setting influences the character in this excerpt.

> She had swum too far out. The waves were higher than she thought. She was struggling hard to get to shore. She wondered if she would make it. She thought of her childhood. Had she been right to run away from home, she wondered? Just then, a lifeguard grabbed her and helped her to shore.

The setting of the ocean and the high waves creates a conflict in the character. She is worried. She thinks about her childhood and her parents. She doesn't know if she will make it to shore. This is how the setting affects the character in this excerpt. Without the high waves and the struggle, she would not become so worried and start to think about her past. She probably would not have questioned herself. This is an example of how a setting influences a character. If the waves had not been high, there probably would not have been a struggle or any self-searching of the swimmer's past.

Historical and Cultural Setting

Historical context influences literature in a number of ways. The style of the author's writing can be impacted by the historical period during which it was written (e.g., Dickens wrote at a time when authors were paid by the word; this is why his novels are so long). Obviously, the setting of the book includes its historical context. In addition, dialect may be a function of the historical period of the book. When a reader understands the historical context of a particular book, he or she can have a deeper understanding of the novel. Knowing about the time period during which the author wrote, as well as the time period discussed in the novel, helps the reader understand some of the author's choices, including character motivations.

Patterns Related to Settings

The setting of a story can allow the reader to draw on personal experience about where the story takes place. If a story takes place on a farm, the reader will likely picture a rural, peaceful setting, which may go along with (or be in contrast to) the actual plot of the story. For example, a reader would not expect a scary story to occur on a farm on a sunny day. Conversely, a reader may view a dark subway as a dangerous place, while the plot of a story set there may be based on a very calm series of events. When an author is crafting a story, they need to consider what the audience may already think about a particular setting in order to properly present the events of a story for greatest impact.

Chapter Quiz

1. Which of the following is the lesson that a story teaches, or the message the author wants to get across?

a. Theme
b. Setting
c. Topic
d. Plot

2. What type of character often gets their characteristics and mannerisms from stereotypes of people that are widely recognized?

a. Minor characters
b. Stock characters
c. Flat characters
d. Round characters

3. Every plot will begin with ___________, which introduces the characters and the setting of the story.

a. Conflict
b. Rising action
c. Foreshadowing
d. Exposition

4. Which of the following would most likely convey a peaceful setting to the reader?

a. Sunny farm
b. Damp basement
c. Loud construction site
d. Dark subway

Chapter Quiz Answer Key

1. A: See section **Theme**

2. B: See section **Stock Characters**

3. D: See section **Plot**

4. A: See section **Patterns Related to Settings**

Literary Genres

Children's Literature

There are types of texts that are specifically meant to be read by children or younger audiences. Children's literature contains many different **genres**, which are categories that texts can be divided into. Some types of children's literature are

- **Folktales** -Songs, stories, myths, or proverbs belonging to a group of people. Often passed down from generation to generation by word of mouth.
- **Fairy tales** are stories that include fictional creatures or characters with fantastical traits and abilities. Fairy tales often end happily and depict the victory of good over evil. The plots and characters in fairy tales are often far-fetched and whimsical.
- **Fables** –Story told (often by a narrator) full of supernatural features like speaking animals. The tale demonstrates a useful truth at the end.
- **Legends** -A story featuring a national or folk hero. Often has a basis in actual fact, but also contains imaginative material.
- **Myth** -A legend or traditional narrative, often based on a historical event. The story reveals something about human behavior or the natural world, and often involves actions of gods.
- **Tall Tales** -A story full of outlandish exaggerations, often humorous and containing heroes who perform impossible acts easily.

Poetry

Poet Versus Speaker

The author of a poem is called a **poet**. Many poems are written in first person, which means the **stanzas** (groups of lines) include words like "I" and "me." However, the poet is not always the **speaker** of the poem. In a novel, the author can create characters with different points of view. The characters can argue or have different roles to play in telling the story. Similarly, a poet may write a poem from a different point of view or even include more than one voice. The speaker is the voice of the poem, and is not always the same person as the poet him or herself. The reader or listener should know that the person telling the story is a character, and not always a real person.

For example, this excerpt from a poem by Dr. Seuss reads:

> When you think things are bad,
> when you feel sour and blue,
> when you start to get mad...
> you should do what I do!
> Just tell yourself, Duckie,
> you're really quite lucky!
> Some people are much more...
> oh, ever so much more...
> oh, muchly much-much more
> unlucky than you!

Even though one line has the word "I" in it, the poem is not from the perspective of Dr. Seuss. He is the author of the poem, but not the speaker. The person saying "I" is a character, just like in a story.

Sensory Language in Poetry

Sensory language is when the author uses descriptive words and specific details that appeal to a reader's senses (sight, touch, taste, hearing, smell, emotion). For example, the author can use scents that the reader is familiar with to help them imagine what the setting of the poem smells and feels like. This use of sensory language is also called **imagery**.

Rhyme in Poetry

Poets use rhymes to help readers understand poems. Words **rhyme** when they sound similar to each other, especially when the similar sound is at the end of the words, like *cat* and *hat*, or *roar* and *soar*. Rhyming words usually have endings that are spelled the same way, but sometimes they are spelled differently, like *wait* and *hate* or *bear* and *snare*.

Famous poet Shel Silverstein uses rhyme in many of his poems. For example, in his poem "Listen to the Mustn'ts", the last word of the first- and second-lines rhyme with each other, and the last word of the third- and fourth-line rhyme with each other.

> Listen to Mustn'ts, child, listen to the Don'ts.
> Listen to the Shouldn'ts, the Impossibles, the Won'ts.
> Listen to the Never Haves, then listen close to me.
> Anything can happen, child, Anything can be.

The pattern of the rhymes in this poem forms a **rhyme scheme**. Sometimes poets use a rhyme scheme that makes every other line of the poem rhyme instead.

Sound Devices

Sound devices allow authors to add another level to their texts by tapping into the spoken part of language. Authors may use many sound devices to create meaning and help readers understand them better, including:

Onomatopoeia

- Appeals to the reader's sense of hearing by using words that copy the noises objects or people make, like sound effects.
- For example, an author might write "The soccer ball whooshed across the field into the goalie's net, scoring the winning point!" The word "whooshed" is an **onomatopoeia** because it mimics the sound of air moving quickly. Because the writer chose to include an onomatopoeia, the reader is able to better picture the action in the sentence.

Alliteration, Assonance, and Consonance

- Alliteration, assonance, and consonance all deal with using the same sound throughout a line or sentence. **Alliteration** is the use of words that begin with the **same sound** in a sentence or in a line of poetry. **Assonance** refers to alliteration with a repeated **vowel** sound, whereas **consonance** refers to alliteration with **consonant** sounds.
- For example, the following line contains two sets of alliteration: "I saw a fly fly past my eye, straight into a fresh cherry pie. I felt a flea flee away from my knee and onto the sleeping dog." The first line uses the same sound in the words *I, fly, eye,* and *pie,* which is assonance. The second line uses both assonance and consonance, using the same vowel sound in *flea, flee, knee*, and, *sleeping*. The repeated consonants show up in the words *felt, flea*, and *flee.*

Review Video: Alliteration in Everyday Expressions
Visit mometrix.com/academy and enter code: 462837

DRAMA

Dramas are texts that are written to be performed by people reading the lines or acting the stories out. They can also be presented as monologues (one character speaks), dialogues (two character speak to each other), or pantomimes (body movements are used instead of spoken words). Dramatic texts are called plays or **scripts**, and they are written differently than other texts.

TEXT STRUCTURE IN DRAMA

Plays are divided into **acts** (large units) and **scenes** (small sections inside acts) instead of chapters. There are also **stage directions**, which are instructions from the playwright about where items go, where actors should move, and what the characters should be doing during the scene. Stage directions are usually in italics to set them apart from other parts of the play. When it is time for a character in a play to speak, there will be **character tag** on the left side of the page which shows the name of the character (all letters of the name are capitalized) followed by a colon.

Here is an example of how a page from a play might look:

Title of Play

Act Number

Scene Number

The setting of the scene is being described here. The reader is being introduced to the characters and the things happening around them. Characters will enter speak to one another during the scene.

CHARACTER 1:

I am speaking. These are words I say. *(stage directions)* I am still speaking.

CHARACTER 2 *enters and does something.*

CHARACTER 2:

Now I am speaking. This is my dialogue.

DIALOGUE AND STAGE DIRECTIONS

Dialogue refers to what the characters say in a play when they are talking to each other, talking to themselves, or even talking to the audience. The type of speech, word choice, and accent a character uses is specific to the role he is playing. For example, a person cast to play a cowboy would have certain words in his vocabulary that a character from a big city in the North would not have.

A playwright also uses stage directions to make the play flow smoothly. Character interaction helps the viewer to understand the mood of the scene. If two characters are confrontational, the viewer is aware that there is some type of conflict occurring. Stage directions create order when all the characters are on stage together.

INFORMATIONAL TEXT

CONTROLLING IDEA

The controlling idea, also called the main idea or thesis, of a passage is usually located in the first paragraph or two of text. Having the controlling idea near the beginning of the passage allows the author to grab the reader's attention and let them know what the rest of the passage will discuss.

To find the controlling idea in a passage, there are questions the reader can ask while reading: What is this passage about? What does the author want the reader to know about the topic? The supporting details will provide evidence that the controlling idea is correct and are found in the body of a passage. The supporting details often provide examples of the controlling idea.

Supporting Details

Provide evidence and backing for the main point. All texts contain details, but they are only classified as supporting details when they serve to reinforce some larger point. Supporting details are most commonly found in informative and persuasive texts. In some cases, they will be clearly indicated with words like **for example** or **for instance**, or they will begin with words like **first**, **second**, and **last**. However, these special words are not a requirement. As a reader, it is important to consider whether the author's supporting details really back up his or her main point. Supporting details can be factual and correct but still not relevant to the author's point. Sometimes, supporting details can seem important but they might not support the main idea in the story well because they are based on opinion that cannot be proven.

Example

Decide whether the following sentence is the main point or a supporting point of a text, and state where the information would be placed in an outline:

> One type of horseback riding, bareback horseback riding, involves sitting on a moving horse without a saddle and grasping the horse's mane.

This sentence is a supporting point, with the main point of the entire text likely about horseback riding in general. As a supporting point, this sentence would go further down in an outline, next to any numeral after numeral I. This sentence can be followed by additional sub-points that further explain the concept of bareback horseback riding. When a supporting point is used to clarify a main point or topic, the supporting point helps to break the topic down into smaller pieces.

Structural Features of Informational Text

Texts which intend to inform the reader about a topic are often accompanied by visual aids or graphics. Some common examples are listed below.

- **Insets and sidebars** show additional information related to the text in boxes or on the sides of the page. Insets can contain pictures or text, and sometimes have different colored backgrounds or font types to make them stand out from the text.
- **Visual aids** include features like diagrams, graphs, and charts. These can help the user think about information in a different way. They do this by visually presenting the relationship between the information in the text.
- **Timelines** are a visual aid which show how events from the text happened over time, and usually contain dates, locations, or other related information.
- **Tables** are visual aids that organize information in a way that shows the relationship between the information. Tables are made using rows and columns, and the pieces in the rows and columns are called cells. Usually, the first row or column will contain a title or heading that categorizes or defines the other cells in that row or column.
- **Bullet points** list items separately, making facts and ideas easier to see and understand.
- **Numbers** can also be used to list separate items. Usually, numbers are used to show that the items are part of a sequence. For example, in a list of instructions, each instruction may be numbered to show the reader the order in which each instruction should be completed.

- **Italics** are a formatting technique that makes text appear slanted. Italics can be used to emphasize text because they cause the text to look different and lead the reader to notice it more easily. Italics are also often used in fiction to show that text is part of a character's thoughts. They are also commonly used to show that a word or section of text is written in a foreign language.
- **Boldface** is a way to format text to make it stand out. Boldface, or bold, text can be used to emphasize a word, phrase, or idea. Boldface can also be used to let the reader know that they can find more information about a term in a glossary, sidebar, or other feature of the text.

Organizational Patterns

Authors want to have an effective text that the reader can understand. If ideas do not follow a **logical order**, the reader will become confused and not know what the author is trying to say. When writing, there are a variety of ways that an author can choose to organize a written work. It is important to choose the pattern that **best presents** the information, as not all patterns will work for every piece of writing. An author may organize ideas according to a timeline, cause and effect, or description of an event or setting.

Order of Importance

The author puts the information in the text in order of what is most important. Order of importance can be either increasing or decreasing, depending on how the writer wants to structure the work.

Chronological Order

The author organizes the progression of events based upon when they occurred and what was included in each step of the story. By organizing the text in this way the author presents all necessary information about the six questions readers can ask to help themselves understand the text: who, what, when, where, why, and how.

Problem and Solution

The author presents some information as a problem and then discusses a solution or attempted solution to that problem. In problem and solution, there is generally one main problem, but that one problem may have several possible solutions.

For example, suppose Billy wants a new video game but does not have the money. There are several possible solutions to this. He might try asking his mom to buy it for him. If that does not work, he could offer to do small jobs to earn enough money to buy it. A third possibility might be to wait until his birthday and ask for it then.

Cause and Effect

The author will write about relationship between two events that occur, where the second event occurs as a result of the first.

For example, a text may discuss a school policy stating that when a student is late to school too many times, they receive a detention. Later in the text, we might see a student repeatedly arriving late to school, after which he is given a detention. In this example, the **cause** is the student being late to school, and the **effect** is the student receiving a detention.

Compare and Contrast

The author will show similarities and differences between items or events.

For example, the author may write about cats and dogs. They might start by giving a brief description of the two. Then they will want to point out all of the similarities, such as; they both have tails, and both are kept as pets. Next, they will explain the differences, such as; dogs are canines, while cats are felines. They will try to provide as much detail as possible about both the similarities and the differences.

Ideas may vary in complexity, in addition to their main point. Topics of debate, or issues, may have pros and cons. By comparing the positive and negative aspects of each view, the reader can better understand how the viewpoints are similar and different.

EXAMPLE

Read the following two viewpoints and compare and contrast how the two viewpoints are similar and different:

> (1) Basketball is the best sport to play, because a participant can be part of a team and excel individually.
>
> (2) In basketball, players must work together to execute plays and achieve points for the team.

In the first viewpoint, the author states that basketball is the best sport to play, whereas in the second viewpoint, the author simply states how the game is played. The first viewpoint also refers to an individual player's performance, while the second viewpoint focuses on the fact that the team needs to score points together in order to win the game. The first viewpoint is trying to convince the reader, while the second viewpoint is explaining how the game is played. Yes, an individual may excel at scoring points, as indicated in the first viewpoint, but the second viewpoint emphasizes the fact that plays need to be done together in order to score points for the entire team. Two differing viewpoints will often overlap in relation to the topic that they are discussing.

IDENTIFYING ORGANIZATIONAL PATTERNS

EXAMPLE

Read the following paragraph from a news story and describe how the author organizes information in the story:

> The parade in honor of the town's 200th anniversary began at the corner of 57th Street at 9:00 a.m. on Saturday morning. Members of the fire department led the parade, dressed in their bright red hats and heavy yellow coats. At 9:15 a.m., members of the high school band gave a performance.

The news story uses chronological order organize ideas. The reader is given information about what type of event occurred, when the event occurred, what the event was about, and who was included.

EXAMPLE

Identify organizational pattern that is used in the following sentence from *Morte d'Arthur* by Sir Thomas Malory:

> The king had given his promise, so he was obliged to agree.

The text structure of cause and effect is used in this sentence. The cause in the sentence is that the king gave his promise, and the effect is that he had to agree.

Argumentative Texts

Identifying the Claim

In a persuasive or argumentative text, the author is writing in order to make and support a claim. A claim is similar to the key idea of an informational text. However, a claim can be argued, which means that some readers may not agree with it. The author of the text will need to use the body of the text to support the claim and show readers why they should agree with it. To identify the claim of a text, first identify the topic. Then, read the introduction text to see what the author writes about the topic.

The claim should be clearly stated in the introduction. However, if the claim is still not clear, read the body to see what kind of evidence the author uses to support the claim. The way that the author gives and applies evidence may also show what the claim of the text is.

Call to Action

Another strategy is to look for a call to action in the text. A call to action is a statement that instructs the reader to do something after reading the text. Often, the call to action will tell the reader to do something that shows that he or she agrees with the author's claim. For example, if an author's claim is that reading is better than watching a movie, the author may include a call to action that says "Turn off the TV and dig in to a new book today!" By including this statement, the author is telling the readers to show their agreement by choosing to read rather than watch a movie.

Identifying How the Author Supports a Claim

In a persuasive or argumentative text, the author must use information to support his or her claim. This information is called evidence. Below are common types of evidence an author may use to support a claim:

- **Facts:** Authors may use facts that show that their claim is true. For example, a claim that fish are better pets than dogs can be supported by the fact that fish cannot make a mess inside a house.
- **Examples:** Authors may give examples of events or experiences that suggest that their claim is true. For example, an author may claim that people should exercise because it will make them healthier. The author could give an example of how exercise can improve a person's health in order to support this claim.
- **Quotes:** An author can support a claim by using quotes from other people or texts. If the person or text makes a statement that shows that the author's claim is true, the author can include that quote in his or her text. When authors include quotes in their work, they must always tell the reader where the quote came from.

The author must use enough evidence to support the claim. If the evidence does not fully support the claim in the text, then the author must continue working to find evidence for the claim. The evidence used to support a claim must also be believable and come from a reliable source.

Identifying the Intended Audience

Authors of persuasive and argumentative texts want to convince others to agree with a claim or take a certain action. Because of this, they will often write to a specific audience. Often, the target audience will include people who disagree with the author's claim. The author's desire is to give these people information that will lead them to change their minds or actions.

Strategies for Identifying the Intended Audience

One way to identify the intended audience of a persuasive or argumentative text is to first identify the author's claim. Then, consider who would disagree with the author's claim. This group of people is likely the group that the author wants to persuade.

Another way to identify the audience is to look for clues in the text. Sometimes, authors will clearly state which people are included in the intended audience. For example, imagine that an author includes the statement, "Teachers should reward their students every time they make a good grade on a test." This shows that the text is written to persuade teachers who do not already reward their students for good test grades. Similarly, a call to action may show who the target audience is by instructing the members of the audience to take a certain action.

Chapter Quiz

1. What type of children's literature can be described as songs, stories, myths, or proverbs belonging to a group of people, that are often passed down from generation to generation by word of mouth?

a. Folktales
b. Fables
c. Legends
d. Tall tales

2. In poetry, which of the following appeals to the reader's sense of hearing by using words that begin with the same consonant sound in a sentence or in a line of poetry?

a. Assonance
b. Rhyme
c. Line breaks
d. Alliteration

3. In dramatic texts (plays or scripts), which of the following are usually in italics to set them apart from other parts of the play?

a. Dialogues
b. Acts and scenes
c. Stage directions
d. Character tags

4. What structural feature is used to list items separately, making facts and ideas easier to see and understand?

a. Boldface
b. Bullet points
c. Sidebars
d. Headings

5. If an author writes about cats and dogs, showing their similarities and differences, this would be an example of what type of organizational pattern?

a. Cause and effect
b. Problem and solution
c. Proposition and support
d. Compare and contrast

6. What sound device appeals to the reader's sense of hearing by using words that copy the noises objects or people make (for example, pow or whoosh)?

a. Onomatopoeia
b. Alliteration
c. Assonance
d. Consonance

Chapter Quiz Answer Key

1. A: See section **Children's Literature**

2. D: See section **Alliteration, Assonance, and Consonance**

3. C: See section **Text Structure in Drama**

4. B: See section **Structural Features of Informational Text**

5. D: See section **Compare and Contrast**

6. A: See section **Onomatopoeia**

Author's Purpose and Craft

Author's Purpose

An author may write a text for many different purposes. Four of the most common purposes are to inform, to persuade or influence, to express, or to entertain readers.

Informational Texts

- Inform the reader on a topic that they previously knew nothing about, such as many non-fiction texts.
- For example, an informative paper on kangaroos would detail where kangaroos live, what they look like, what they eat, and other habits.
- Informational texts are usually non-fiction, such as articles or instructions. They usually follow structures such as order of importance, problem and solution, or compare and contrast.

Persuasive Texts

- Influence the reader to think a certain way about a topic, calling them to action or pointing them toward resources that would help them to learn more about the topic.
- For example, an author may try to persuade the reader that waterparks are the best place to go in the summer when it is hot outside. The author would present information about waterparks and explain *why* they are good places to visit.
- Persuasive texts can be either fiction or non-fiction. They usually follow a structure such as proposal and support or cause and effect.

Expressive Texts

- Express the author or speaker's opinion or emotions about a topic. Lots of descriptive words are used to clearly show the reader how the author or speaker feels.
- For example, the author may think that a new playground in town is a good idea, and write an essay about why a playground would be great for the community.

ENTERTAINING TEXTS

- Entertain the reader, such as in most fictional texts.
- For example, Astrid Lindren, the author of *Pippi Longstocking*, entertains her readers with the story of a year in the life of a young girl named Pippilotta, who goes on wild adventures with her horse and a monkey named Mr. Nilsson.
- Entertaining texts can be either fiction or non-fiction, but are usually stories such as a fairy tale or fictional piece of writing. Entertaining texts usually follow a chronological order.

Authors usually write to entertain, to inform, or to persuade their readers. The organization structure or pattern they use is related to what the author's purpose is. It is important to choose the pattern that best presents the information, as not all patterns will work for every piece of writing.

EXAMPLE

Read the following sentence. State the author's point in writing the sentence, whether it is to inform, persuade, express an opinion, or entertain:

> The rollercoaster reached a peak and paused for a second, before gliding down the other side of the hill with a roar.

The purpose of the sentence is to entertain the reader. The author does not state his or her opinion on the topic, and the sentence doesn't inform the reader about an important topic. The sentence does not persuade the reader to accept a certain point of view, and is instead meant to entertain the reader by giving them the feeling they might get from riding an exciting roller coaster.

Notice that the text describes an event, rather than an issue or conflict. The event is part of a larger tale, where a series of events occur to form an entire story. The reader may notice that the author uses descriptive words to present the setting, such as gliding and roar. The reader can better picture a story when the setting is clearly presented.

EXAMPLE

Read the following sentence and state the author's point in writing the sentence, whether it is to inform, entertain, persuade, or state an opinion:

> The new student handbook makes it against the rules to wear roller skates inside the school buildings.

The purpose of this sentence is to inform the reader. The sentence does not state an opinion on the topic, nor is it meant to entertain the reader. The sentence also does not persuade the reader to accept a certain point of view. The sentence gives information to the reader that they need to know in order to avoid breaking the rules.

EXAMPLE

Read the following sentence from *Esperanza Rising* by Pam Munoz Ryan and state the author's purpose in writing the sentence: whether it is to inform, entertain, persuade, or state an opinion:

> "Our Land is alive, Esperanza...This whole valley breathes and lives..." He picked up a handful of earth and studied it. "Did you know that when you lie down on the land, you can feel it breathe? That you can feel its heart beating."

The purpose of the sentence is to entertain the reader. The sentence does not tell the reader important information about a specific topic, it is simply used as part of a greater fictional story meant for entertainment, in this case, about a legend that the land is alive. The sentence does not persuade the reader to accept a certain point of view, nor does it state an opinion.

When an author wishes to persuade the reader to accept a certain point of view, evidence is used to back-up a claim. If the author wants to state an opinion, that opinion is included within the text. Sentences that are meant to inform contain facts that the reader needs to know and are not often found in fictional stories.

PRINT AND GRAPHIC FEATURES

An author may show information in a chart, a graph, in paragraph format, or as a list. Information may also be shown in a picture or a diagram. The way an author chooses to show information is often based on the purpose of the text and the audience that the text is meant to reach.

A reader may be asked to answer questions based on the graphic by itself, how the graphic relates to the text, or how the text would best be shown in a graphic form. Some common examples of graphics are cause and effect organizers, circle graphs, bar graphs, illustrations, and diagrams.

CAUSE AND EFFECT GRAPHIC ORGANIZERS

Cause-and-effect graphic organizers are often used to map the **elements of a story**. A reader might read a story about a string of events and then be asked to correctly fill in either the **cause** or **effect** of an event in the story.

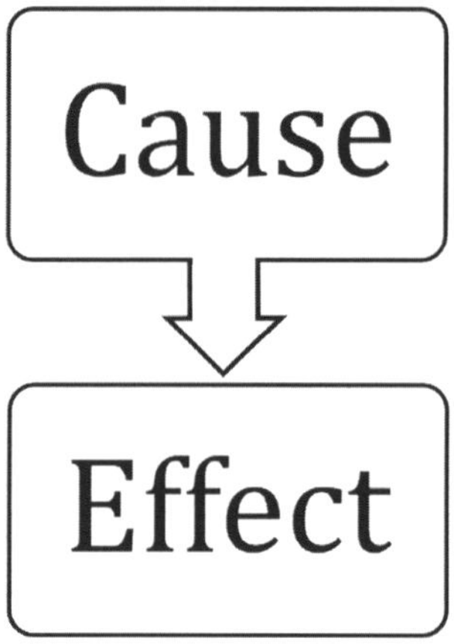

EXAMPLE

Read the following excerpt from *Ramona Quimby, Age 8* by Beverly Cleary and decide what the cause of the hectic morning at the Quimby house is.

> With all four members of the family leaving at different times in different directions, mornings were flurried in the Quimby household.

A **cause and effect** graphic organizer for this excerpt might look something like this:

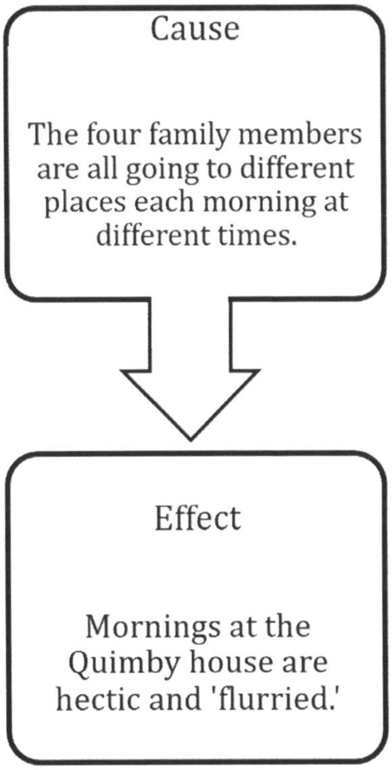

Circle Graphs

Circle graphs, also called pie charts, are often used to represent information that can be shown as **parts of a whole**. For example, this graph shows the results of people being asked about their favorite color:

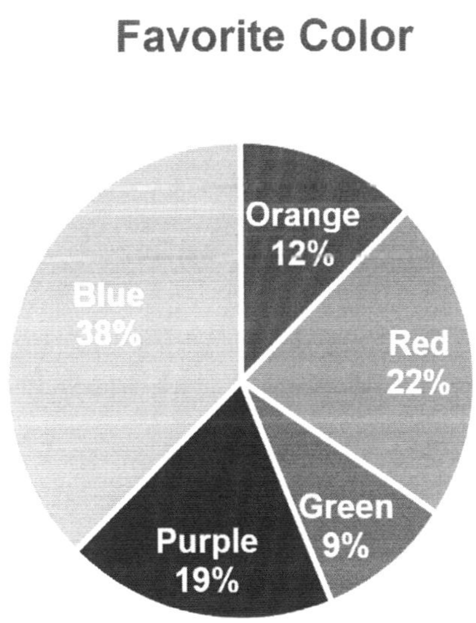

Bar Graphs

Bar graphs are used to show information about **numbers**. For example, this graph is a different way of representing the same results as those in the circle graph.

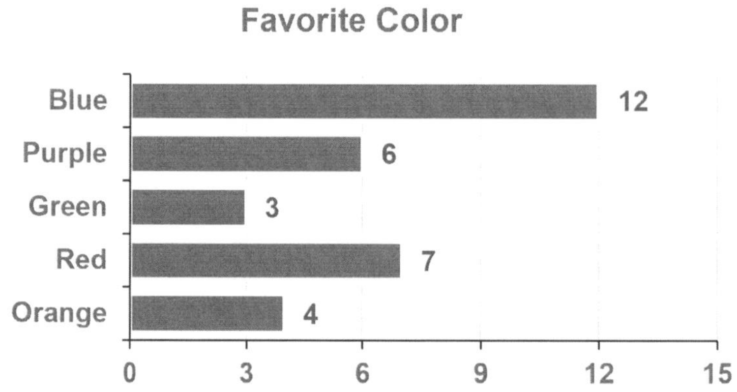

Illustrations and Photographs

Authors may choose to include **illustrations** or **photographs** (or both) with their texts. These two image types both show something from the text or give more information about the text.

Illustrations are drawings of an object. They may be based on reality, or they may represent an artist's abstract idea. For example, this is an illustration of a 1903 automobile:

Photographs are pictures of objects. They are generally extremely realistic, and most often show an object as it actually existed at that moment in time. For example, this is a photograph of a 1917 automobile:

Both illustrations and photographs give the reader another way to relate to and understand the text. The reader may be asked how the image relates to the text, what type of caption the image should be given, or why the author chose to include the image with the text.

Diagrams

Diagrams are used to show information in a visual way. There are many different types of diagrams, including:

Diagrams that show the parts of an object, how they work together, or how they should be put together. This is an example of a diagram which shows how gears turn together

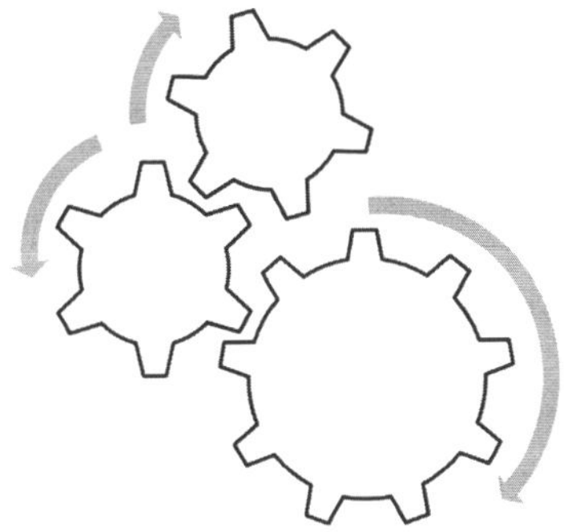

Diagrams that show how information is related are called **Venn Diagrams**. These are ways to visually see the way in which two different ideas overlap. This is an example of a Venn Diagram comparing cats and dogs:

IMAGERY

Imagery is the use of **descriptive language** to add life or feeling to a work of literature. Many authors add literary and sound devices to create vivid pictures in the minds of their readers. Most of the time, imagery is thought to be one of the best ways to help readers fully understand and remember a work.

The most common forms of imagery are those that appeal to the sense of sight and sound. Imagery that appeals to the sense of sight, or **visual imagery**, helps the reader picture an event in their mind, usually by including specific details in the text that are not strictly necessary for the purpose of the story, but allow the reader to more easily "see" the scene. Some common forms of figurative language can help create visual imagery.

Review Video: Sensory Language
Visit mometrix.com/academy and enter code: 177314

LITERAL AND FIGURATIVE LANGUAGE

Many types of text use both **literal language**, which means just what it says, and **figurative language**, which means something more than the literal words being used. Figurative language is a literary device that allows the author to expand reality in a vivid way. When an author uses figurative language, she connects things in an exaggerated way in order to create a memorable image, which helps to describe a situation in a new way for the reader.

Review Video: Figurative Language
Visit mometrix.com/academy and enter code: 584902

Simile

- Shows similarity between two ideas or objects, using the words "**like**" or "**as**"
- For example, an author might write "The princess is as beautiful as a rose" to compare the appearance of a woman to a beautiful flower.

Metaphor

- Puts one idea in place of another to draw a parallel between the two ideas.
- For example, an author might write "Her room was a pigsty," to compare a person's bedroom to a dirty spot where pigs sleep.

Symbolism

- Using one object to stand for something else.
- For example, an author may include a flag flying high throughout a story to show pride in the characters' country and to represent the idea of patriotism.

Hyperbole

- An extreme exaggeration of an idea.
- For example, a character might say "I'm starving to death!" to show that they are really hungry. Most of the time a character who says this is not literally going to die from hunger, they are just ready for a snack.

Irony

- Uses sarcasm or humor (usually with an emphasis on the opposite) to show difference from literal meaning.
- For example, if a character says "Well today must be my lucky day!" after they left their homework on the kitchen table, they are being ironic. The irony used here helps show that it is definitely *not* the character's lucky day.

Personification

- Gives life or human characteristics to an inanimate object
- For example, if an author writes "The trees whispered to each other across the wide blue sky," they are using personification to help the reader imagine the scene. Trees are not human beings, so they do not whisper, but the image created in the reader stands out more than a literal description would.

Example

Based on current knowledge, identify whether metaphor, simile, or hyperbole is used in this sentence:

> The chiming bell was a beacon of hope for the downtrodden villagers.

A metaphor is used in this sentence to draw a parallel between "the chiming bell" and "a beacon of hope." The bell is being compared to something else in the sentence, which indicates the use of metaphor or simile, but the reader knows that the sentence does not contain a simile, because the words **like** and **as** are not used to show the comparison. The sentence also does not contain an exaggeration of facts, so the reader can see that hyperbole is not used.

Point of View

Authors choose which character tells the story they are writing. This is called **point of view**. The point of view affects the story in many ways. There are three general types of point of view:

First Person

- Tells a story through the eyes of one character.
- Uses the pronouns 'I,' 'me,' 'we,' and 'my.'
- The reader gets only one side of the story, without any other angles on what may have happened in the text

Second Person

- Tells a story using the pronoun 'you.'
- The least common point of view.

Third Person

- Tells a story about a character or group of characters from an outside viewpoint.
- Uses the words 'her', 'his,' 'they,' or a name to talk about a character or characters.
- A common way to show action in a story which allows the author to easily and realistically tell a story from more than one person's viewpoint.
- Gives readers a more complete view of a story as it is told from many different perspectives.
    - Gives readers a more complete view of a story as it is told from many different perspectives.

Stereotypes and Anecdotes

Sometimes authors will use devices that are based on their own or others' experiences to try to make a text more believable or relatable. An **anecdote** is a brief story authors may use to help the reader relate to the author or his or her purpose for writing. Anecdotes can illustrate the author's point a way that is more real, believable, and relatable to the reader. A **stereotype** is a generalization, or assumption, about a specific group of people. Authors can use stereotypes to help a reader understand that a character has a certain set of qualities and traits.

Style and Voice

Style and voice play an important role in the development of a story. The reader's impression of a story can vary based on the style and voice used by the author. **Style** refers to the way an author uses words, phrases, and sentence structure. The style of the text can change depending on whether the author uses short, choppy sentences, long, elaborate sentences, formal language, or informal language. **Voice** refers to the characteristics of a text that show the author's personality and distinguish the author from other writers. An author's voice may be recognized through the way they use words or the way they organize and present their thoughts. Voice is specific to each writer, and it can be as specific and unique as personality.

Chapter Quiz

1. An author's purpose in writing fiction is most often to:

a. Persuade
b. Inform
c. Entertain
d. Express

2. What is the least common point of view, that tells a story using the pronouns "you"?

a. First person
b. Second person
c. Third person
d. Narrator

3. What type of graphic can be used to visually see the way in which two different ideas overlap?

a. Circle graph
b. Bar graph
c. Venn diagram
d. Cause and effect organizer

4. What common form of figurative language puts one idea in place of another to draw a parallel between the two ideas?

a. Metaphor
b. Simile
c. Hyperbole
d. Irony

Chapter Quiz Answer Key

1. C: See section **Author's Purpose**

2. B: See section **Second Person**

3. C: See section **Diagrams**

4. A: See section **Metaphor**

Writing

Spelling

Vowels and Consonants

Vowels and consonants describe the sounds in the English language. **Vowels** are the sounds made with only the voice, such as /a/, /e/, /i/, /o/, and /u/. Sometimes the letter y can make an /i/ sound. Consonants make up all of the other sounds in English. Consonants are sounded out by using the tongue, teeth, and lips.

Syllables

Syllables are the individual sounds that make up spoken words. Syllables can be determined by saying a word out loud and listening to what the individual sounds are. Some people split sounds up differently, but the important part of syllables is knowing where each sound in a word starts and stops.

One Syllable	Two Syllable	Three Syllable	Four Syllable
Bat	Draw-ing	Ba-tter-y	Com-for-ta-ble
Car	Foot-ball	Com-put-er	In-vis-i-ble
Home	Wa-ter	Flam-in-go	Wat-er-mel-on

Sometimes, words are diagrammed using the letters v and c to describe the vowels and consonants in the word. This helps to determine what types of syllables the word contains.

	Closed Syllables	Open Syllables	VCe Syllables
Word	Cat	Banana	Ripe
Pronunciation	/Kat/	/Buh-Na-Nuh/	/Rīp/
Syllables	CVC	CV-CV-CV	CVC

Notice how in the first example, cat is one syllable, which is made up of a consonant sound from the letter c, a vowel from the letter a, and another consonant sound from the letter t. In the second example, banana is three syllables, each of which has a consonant followed by a vowel.

Closed Syllables

Closed syllables are the easiest to recognize. They are marked by a consonant sound closing off the beginning or end of a syllable.

Open Syllables

Open syllable refers to the beginning or end of a syllable that does not have a consonant closing it off. Examples of this include the words *egg* and *blue.* The number and placement of consonants in different open syllables can affect the way the vowel is pronounced in each syllable.

	VCCV	VCV
Word	Tennis, Method	Robin, Tiger
Pronunciation	/Ten-is/, /Meth-od /	/Rob-in/, /Tī-ger/
Syllables	VC/CV, VCC/V	VC/V, V/CV

VCe Syllables

VCe syllables refer to words that have a silent e in them. The letter e is included to help identify the word when reading it, but the e sound is not spoken. Examples of words with silent e sounds are *bite, cake, flute,* and *tube.*

VV Syllables

When two vowels appear next to each other in a word, they may work together to make a single sound. However, when the vowels do not make one sound together, they mark the end of one syllable and the beginning of another syllable. These are VV syllables, also called vowel teams. For example, *duel, flour,* and *diary* all contain VV syllables.

R-Controlled Vowel Syllables

R-controlled syllables are formed when an *r* comes after a vowel. In r-controlled syllables, the vowel is paired with the *r* and makes a unique sound. Examples of words with r-controlled syllables are *jar, teacher, fir, torn,* and *spur.*

Final Stable Syllables

When a word ends in a Cle syllable, or a consonant followed by *le,* it has a final stable syllable. The syllable is made of these three letters. Examples of words with final stable syllables are *spectacle, thimble,* and *giggle.*

Affixes and Root Words

Affixes are syllables attached to the beginning or end of a word to adjust its meaning. Both prefixes and suffixes are affixes. A **prefix** is a syllable that appears at the beginning of a word that adjusts the root, or base, word' s meaning. For example, the prefix *mis* means wrong. When combined with the root word *spelling,* the word *misspelling* is created, which means wrong spelling. A **root word** is the base of a word that can have affixes added to it. For example, the suffix *-er* can be added to the root word *manage* to create *manager,* which means a person or thing who manages. The suffix -*able,* meaning capable of, can be added to *manage* to create *managable,* which means capable of being managed. Keep in mind that not every prefix and suffix can be simply added to a root word, since adding an affix will sometimes require some other spelling changes for the root word.

Common Prefixes

Prefix	Definition	Examples
anti-	against, opposing	antigravity, antidote
com-	with, together, very	community, combine
de-	from	depart, detangle
dis-	away, off, down, not	dislike, disappear

Prefix	Definition	Examples
ex-	out	extract, exterior
inter-	among, between	intersection, interstate
mis-	bad, poorly, not	mistake, misspell, misunderstand
non-	not	nonexistent, nonsense
over-	above, in excess	overdone, overhead
post-	after, following	postpone, postscript
pre-	before, previous	prevent, premade
pro-	forward, in place of	propel, pronoun
retro-	back, backward	retrospect, retrograde
semi-	half, partly	semicircle, semicolon
sub-	under, beneath	submarine, subject
super-	above, extra	superstore, supervise
re-	backward, again	repeat, redo
trans-	across, beyond, over	transform, transport, transit
un-	not, reverse of	unhappy, unlock
uni-	one	uniform, unity

COMMON SUFFIXES

Suffix	Definition	Examples
-able or -ible	capable of being	suitable, edible
-ation	action, state, result	occupation, federation, starvation
-dom	state, rank, condition	kingdom, wisdom
-en	cause to be, become	deepen, strengthen
-er or -or	role, function	teacher, elevator
-ess	feminine	waitress, actress
-ful	filled with, marked by	thankful, hateful
-hood	state, condition	falsehood, statehood
-ion	action, result, state	union, confusion
-ish	suggesting, like	feverish, childish
-ist	worker, status, follower	dentist, finalist, colonist
-ity or -ty	state, quality, condition	ability, faulty
-ize	cause to be, treat as	realize, emphasize
-less	lacking, without	hopeless, countless
-ment	result, action	refreshment, employment
-ness	quality, state	greatness, dullness
-ous	marked by, given to	religious, gracious
-ship	status, relationship, trait	penmanship, friendship

SPELLING CHANGES WITH SUFFIXES

When a suffix is added to the root word, usually the resulting word is spelled just like the root word and the suffix put together. However, there are some words that will require other spelling changes when a suffix is added. These changes include doubling consonants, removing *e*, and changing *y* to *i*.

DOUBLE CONSONANTS

Most words that end in a closed syllable with one closing consonant will need the final consonant doubled if a suffix is being added.

Adding -ing: fibbing, submitting, running

Adding -er: sadder, flipper, hummer

Adding -est: biggest, flattest, hippest

Removing E

Many words ending with a VCe syllable will lose the silent *e* when a suffix is added. This only applies if the first letter of the suffix is a vowel.

Root Words Ending in Y

If the root word ends with a consonant and a *y,* when a suffix is added, an *i* will replace the *y.*

Adding -ness: silliness, readiness, stickiness

Adding -ous: glorious, studious, industrious

Adding -ed: applied, satisfied, spied

Pronunciation Changes with Suffixes

Suffixes may change the way that letters are pronounced when a word is read aloud. It is important to know how to spell these words when adding suffixes, especially if the spelling does not seem to match the pronunciation.

For example, consider the suffixes *-ian* and *-ion*. When a word ends in *c*, *s*, or *t* and one of these two suffixes is added to it, the word may be pronounced with a *sh* or *zh* sound. However, the word will still be spelled using the *c*, *s*, or *t*.

> Examples with -ian: electric + ian=electrician | Egypt + ian=Egyptian
>
> Examples with -ion: fuse + ion=fusion | intersect + ion=intersection

Common Spelling Mistakes

Vowels

There must be a vowel in every word. If a writer spells a word without a vowel, he or she has made a mistake and should correct it. Not every word needs a consonant, and there are even some words that are made of one vowel, like *a* or *I*. If a word has more than one syllable, there should also be at least one vowel in every syllable. However, there are words and syllables that do not contain *a*, *e*, *i*, *o*, and *u*. In these words and syllables, *y* acts as a vowel.

I Before E

If a word contains the letters *i* and *e* right next to each other, the *i* usually goes before the *e*, such as in *relieve*. However, if the two letters come right after a *c*, then the *e* should go before the *i*, such as in *receipt*. Also, if the two letters make a long *a* sound when spoken aloud, the *e* should go before the *i*, such as in *their*. Several words do not follow these rules, so it is best to double-check the spelling of confusing words in the dictionary.

Word Confusion

To, Too, and Two

To can be an adverb or a preposition for showing direction, purpose, and relationship. A dictionary can also be used to see the many other ways to use *to* in a sentence.

> Examples: I went to the store. | I want to go with you.

Too is an adverb that means *also, as well, very,* or *in excess.*

Examples: I can walk a mile too. | You have eaten too much.

Two is a number.

Example: You have two minutes left.

THERE, THEIR, AND THEY'RE

There can be an adjective, adverb, or pronoun. Often, *there* is used to show a place or to start a sentence.

Examples: I went there yesterday. | There is something in his pocket.

Their is a pronoun that is used to show ownership.

Examples: He is their father. | This is their fourth apology this week.

They're is a contraction of *they are.*

Example: Did you know that they're in town?

ITS AND IT'S

Its is a possessive pronoun that shows ownership.

Example: The guitar is in its case.

It's is a contraction of *it is.*

Example: It's an honor and a privilege to meet you.

AFFECT AND EFFECT

There are two main reasons that *affect* and *effect* are so often confused: 1) both words can be used as either a noun or a verb, and 2) unlike most homophones, their usage and meanings are closely related to each other. Here is a quick explanation of the four usage options:

Affect (n): feeling, emotion, or mood that is displayed

Example: The patient had a flat *affect.* (i.e., his face showed little or no emotion)

Affect (v): to alter, to change, to influence

Example: The sunshine *affects* the plant's growth.

Effect (n): a result, a consequence

Example: What *effect* will this weather have on our schedule?

Effect (v): to bring about, to cause to be

Example: These new rules will *effect* order in the office.

Chapter Quiz

1. Which of the following words has three syllables?

a. Invisible
b. Battery
c. Drawing
d. Football

2. When a word ends in a Cle syllable, or a consonant followed by *le* (for example, spectacle, thimble, or giggle), it has what type of syllable?

a. VCe syllable
b. VV syllable
c. Final stable syllable
d. R-controlled syllable

3. All of the following prefixes can mean "not" EXCEPT for:

a. dis-
b. ex-
c. non-
d. un-

4. When adding a suffix to most words that end in a closed syllable with one closing consonant (for example, sad or flip), what change needs to be made to the root word?

a. No change is needed
b. Add a y before the suffix
c. Add a silent e
d. Double the final consonant

5. If a word contains the letters *i* and *e* right next to each other, the *i* usually goes before the *e*, EXCEPT when the two letters come right after:

a. C
b. F
c. N
d. T

6. There, they're, and their are commonly misspelled homophones. Which one is a pronoun that is used to show ownership?

a. There
b. They're
c. Their
d. All of the above

Chapter Quiz Answer Key

1. B: See section **Syllables**

2. C: See section **Final Stable Syllables**

3. B: See section **Common Prefixes**

4. D: See section **Double Consonants**

5. A: See section **I Before E**

6. C: See section **There, Their, and They're**

Writing Process

Brainstorming

When choosing what to write about, activities like brainstorming can help inspire new ideas or help writers see how their ideas go together. **Brainstorming** means considering a variety of topics or ideas and is mainly used to find a creative approach to a subject or problem. A good first step in brainstorming is simple **free-association** with a topic. One way of doing this is sitting down with paper and pen and writing every thought that comes to mind about the topic in a word or phrase. It does not matter how helpful or good the thought seems at first; the writer should write down everything that comes to mind about the topic. Then, the writer should read the list over a few times. Next, he or she should look for patterns, repetitions, and clusters of ideas. This allows a variety of fresh ideas to come as the writer thinks about the topic.

Free Writing

Free writing is a more organized form of brainstorming. **Free writing** means taking a limited amount of time, like 2 to 3 minutes, to write everything that comes to mind about a topic in complete sentences. When the time is up, the writer should review everything he or she has written down. Many of the sentences may not make sense, but they may contain ideas and details that help the writer organize his or her ideas and prepare to plan the composition. Usually, free writing results in more useful ideas than brainstorming because the writer's thoughts and connections are written in complete sentences. However, both methods can be used together to help the writer prepare to plan and write a composition.

Mapping

Mapping an essay describes a couple of different methods. One method is using a graphic organizer with different tiers of ideas and details. The other method is similar to outlining. Outlining usually means using a bulleted list to plan the purpose or main idea for each paragraph in an essay. Under each paragraph bullet, any details, ideas, or sources that are essential to that paragraph will be listed. Most outlines also include a working thesis at the beginning of the outline. The main difference between using an outline and mapping an essay is that mapping does not necessarily mean organizing information by paragraph. The process of mapping an essay will generally include many steps to an outline, such as beginning with a thesis and using a bulleted list, but each point will not always represent one paragraph. This can be very helpful for essay planning because it allows writers to see how their ideas flow and allows them to consider the structure of the essay and make some changes before they begin writing.

Planning

Planning is the process of organizing a piece of writing before writing a draft. At the beginning of planning, writers should decide **why they are writing** and **who will read what they write**. The writer must also choose a **genre**, which is the **type** of composition he or she will write. There are fiction genres, such as comedy, folklore, action, and mystery. There are also nonfiction genres, such as essays, reports, poems, and journals. To plan his or her composition, a writer may create an outline or a graphic organizer, such as a Venn diagram, a spider-map, or a flowchart. These methods should help the writer choose their topic, main ideas, and how to organize the composition. If the writer needs to do research for the composition, he or she may also do so as they plan. Planning helps writers organize all of their ideas and decide if they have enough information to begin their first draft. However, writers should remember that the decisions they make during planning may change later, so their plan does not have to be perfect.

DRAFTING

Writers may then use their plan, outline, or graphic organizer to compose their first draft. They may write more drafts after the first one to improve their writing. Writing multiple drafts can help writers think of different ways to state their ideas and correct mistakes that may be hard to fix without rewriting a section of the composition, or the whole composition. There is no "right" number of drafts, so different writers may write a different number of drafts. Writing drafts also makes it easier to write freely because a writer can improve his or her composition with each draft they write.

REVISING, EDITING, AND PROOFREADING

Once a writer completes a draft, he or she can move on to revising, editing, and proofreading to improve the draft. **Revising** is making sure that the composition is right for the audience, is not missing important information, is on topic, and is well organized. Revising may happen after the first draft so that errors are not repeated in the next draft. Each draft should be revised before the next one is written so that no mistakes are missed. **Editing** comes next. Editing a composition includes steps like improving transitions between paragraphs and making sure each paragraph is on topic. While editing, the writer must pay attention to the words he or she uses and the way the information in each paragraph is organized. Writers may also fix grammar mistakes in the editing phase, since some errors will require a writer to rewrite large parts of their work. **Proofreading** means fixing misspelled words, errors in grammar, and any other small mistakes in the composition.

During the revising, editing, and proofreading steps, it can be helpful for writers to ask a peer to read their work, since he or she may notice mistakes or problems the writer missed before. A writer may also choose to read his or her own work aloud, or listen to someone else read it. Hearing a composition aloud can help writers find mistakes or opportunities for improvement in their work more easily. This happens because when something is read aloud, the person reading the text must pay closer attention to the words on the page. When a writer or a peer reads the composition, they should point out any sentence that confuses them the first time they read it. Most of these sentences can be revised in a way that makes it easier to read and understand.

ADDING AND REMOVING INFORMATION

While both revising and editing may involve changing the words in a composition, they can also involve adding or taking away words. When a writer has completed a draft and reread it, he or she may notice that something, such as a transition, important details, or an explanatory sentence, is missing. Simply changing the words to make the passage sound better will not solve this problem, so the writer must **add** whatever words and information is needed to make the passage make sense and achieve the writer's purpose.

In other cases, a writer may have words, a sentence, or sometimes an entire paragraph that gives unnecessary information or explains the information in a way that is confusing. When this happens, the extra words and information weaken the composition and must be **removed**. Sometimes, this is difficult for writers to do because it may require them to remove writing they are proud of or a fact they find interesting. Despite this, revising and editing are steps meant to improve and strengthen a composition, so the writer should change, add, or remove parts of his or her writing in a way that makes it better and achieves his or her purpose.

Revising Sentences

Sentence variety is important to consider when writing an essay. A variety of sentence lengths and types can make an essay more engaging, and different types of sentences can sometimes help readers better understand information. For example, a sentence containing a list may make more sense when written with a simple sentence structure, since writing a compound sentence containing a list may give the reader too much information at once. On the other hand, information that is closely related and can be connected with a conjunction should be written in a compound sentence, rather than a simple sentence, since a compound sentence helps the reader see that the information goes together.

Using only simple sentences often makes writing boring and bothersome to read. Writing using only compound sentences makes it difficult for writers to explain information well and difficult for readers to understand, since every sentence will include a coordinating conjunction. To check an essay for sentence variety, it is helpful to look at whether the essay contains different sentence structures and lengths. It is also important to pay attention to the way each sentence starts and avoid beginning with the same words or phrases.

Revising Vocabulary

When writing informational or argumentative texts, it is important to use **precise vocabulary**, or **word choice**, to explain your main idea and supporting details. Generalized vocabulary will not help the audience fully understand the points that you are attempting to make because it will not accurately explain your main idea and supporting details. Precise vocabulary is important to use because it will accurately describe the ideas that are central to your text. When you research a subject, make sure to familiarize yourself with any vocabulary that is involved in its explanation. Use context clues, dictionaries, or, if necessary, a technical dictionary to decode any words that you are not familiar with. Precise vocabulary also impacts the effectiveness of narrative text. Carefully choosing vocabulary to describe sensory details, or imagery, helps writers paint the best possible picture of the events they are describing through their writing.

Chapter Quiz

1. Which of the following means taking a limited amount of time, like 2 to 3 minutes, to write everything that comes to mind about a topic in complete sentences?

a. Brainstorming
b. Drafting
c. Mapping
d. Free writing

2. What is often the first step after a writer completes a draft, and involves making sure that the composition is right for the audience, it is not missing important information, is on topic, and is well organized?

a. Adapting
b. Editing
c. Proofreading
d. Revising

3. When revising sentences in an essay, which of the following is NOT good advice?

a. Avoid beginning sentences with the same words or phrases
b. Include a variety of sentence lengths
c. Improve understanding by only using compound sentences
d. Keep sentences simple when they include lists

4. In what step of the writing process does the writer decide why they are writing, who will read what they write, and what genre they want to write?

a. Brainstorming
b. Drafting
c. Mapping
d. Planning

Chapter Quiz Answer Key

1. D: See section **Free Writing**

2. D: See section **Revising, Editing, and Proofreading**

3. C: See section **Revising Sentences**

4. D: See section **Planning**

Essay Structure and Organization

Controlling Ideas and Supporting Details

In the first paragraph of a composition, writers include a sentence that explains the **controlling idea.** This sentence is also known as the **thesis**. The rest of the paragraph shows the reader why the topic of the essay is interesting and includes details that support the controlling idea. One way to understand the relationship between the controlling idea and supporting information is to think about a table: the tabletop is the controlling idea, and each of the table's legs is a supporting detail or group of details. All of the legs work together to support the tabletop and create a table, just like the supporting details work together to support the controlling idea and create a composition.

Introduction

The introduction is used to capture the reader's attention and announce the essay's controlling idea. Normally, the introduction contains about 3-5 sentences. An introduction can begin with an interesting quote, a question, a strong opinion, or something else that will **interest** the reader's and prompt them to keep reading. If the composition has a prompt, the introduction should **restate** or **summarize** some part of the prompt so that the reader will have an idea of what information will be in the essay. Finally, your introduction should include the **controlling idea**, the primary thing the essay will tell the reader.

Review Video: Introduction
Visit mometrix.com/academy and enter code: 961328

Body

In an essay's introduction, the writer states the controlling idea and prepares the reader for the information in the rest of the composition. In the body of the composition, the writer **explains**, **demonstrates**, and **gives more information about** the **controlling idea**. This is done using supporting details and examples that are relevant to the controlling idea of the composition. For example, if the composition's controlling idea is a vacation the writer took, the body will include descriptions of where the writer went, what they experienced, and what they thought of the trip. If the composition's controlling idea is the writer's opinion, the body will include examples and facts that show why he or she has formed that opinion. If composition's controlling idea is a topic and the writer wants to instruct the reader, the body will contain facts, explanations, and examples that help teach the reader about the controlling idea. A writer will use supporting details to explain the controlling idea throughout the body.

The body should also contain multiple paragraphs, and the order the writer puts these paragraphs in is important. Each paragraph should include at least one supporting detail, but a paragraph may include more than one if two or more supporting details work together to support the controlling idea. If the controlling idea is to describe something that happened, the paragraphs should match the order in which the events occurred. If the controlling idea is to present an opinion or instruct the reader, the paragraphs should be ordered in the way that would make the most sense to the reader. The order of body paragraphs is important because it can impact how easy a composition is to read.

Review Video: Drafting Body Paragraphs
Visit mometrix.com/academy and enter code: 724590

Paragraphs

After the introduction of a passage, the body paragraphs will explain and elaborate upon the controlling idea. While each paragraph should relate to the controlling idea of the composition, each paragraph should focus on one point or supporting detail. Normally, a paragraph has a good topic sentence that summarizes the paragraph's main point. A topic sentence is a sentence that gives an introduction to the paragraph and its contents. Topic sentences should contain information that is more specific than what is in the introduction and may include a supporting detail, but they should not contain explanations or examples.

Supporting Details

The next sentences in the paragraph should support the topic sentence. These sentences can contain examples, explanations, or other specific information that supports the topic sentence, which supports the controlling idea of the composition. While a paragraph may be structured in any way, as long as it logically provides information that supports the controlling idea, it can be best to use a template or pattern to make sure that each paragraph is complete and well organized. For example, a good template to follow is topic sentence, evidence, explanation, conclusion. This means that after the topic sentence, the next sentence should provide evidence, such as a quote or example, that shows that the supporting detail is true or relevant. Next, the paragraph should include a sentence that explains how the evidence supports the paragraph's main point. If there are multiple examples or quotes, more than one sentence may be used for each section. Finally, there should be a sentence that concludes the paragraph. The concluding sentence may be similar to the topic sentence, but it should help the reader understand the paragraph and prepare them for the next one.

Choosing Supporting Details and Examples

When writing an informative or argumentative text, writers must choose supporting details carefully. Including details that are irrelevant, inaccurate, or vague does not strengthen the author's writing, while relevant, accurate, provable, and specific details do strengthen the author's writing. These details can make the writer's meaning clearer or give evidence that the author's points are true or logical. Such details may include examples or facts, such as statistics, statements from others who have authority on the subject, and common events or experiences. Choosing appropriate supporting details can also help the author show that they put effort into forming their ideas. This can also make the composition more intriguing and enjoyable to read, since the writer's own interest and insight will be apparent to the reader.

Length of a Paragraph

A paragraph must contain enough information to support its main point and the composition's controlling idea. A paragraph of two or three sentences will most likely not support the main point or controlling idea because it is not likely to contain enough information, explanation, or evidence. When a paragraph does not support the main point or controlling idea, it does not help the writer achieve their purpose or goal for writing the essay. A helpful, informative paragraph will often have somewhere from three to five sentences.

Starting a New Paragraph

For most forms of writing, you will need to use multiple paragraphs. This means that deciding when to start a new paragraph is very important. Reasons for starting a new paragraph include:

- To separate the introduction and conclusion from the body paragraphs
- To move from one supporting detail or point to another
- To indicate an important shift in time or place
- To show a comparison, contrast, or cause and effect relationship

Transitions

Transitions between sentences and paragraphs guide readers from idea to idea and show relationships between sentences and paragraphs. Writers should use transitions carefully and only when they are truly helpful. They should also be selected to fit the author's purpose. Transitions can show relationships such as time, comparison, an order of events, and cause and effect. Transitions are often used at the beginning of a phrase, sentence, or paragraph, since this helps prepare the reader for the next piece of information.

Types of Transitional Words

Time	Afterward, immediately, earlier, meanwhile, recently, lately, now, since, soon, when, then, until, before, etc.
Sequence	too, first, second, further, moreover, also, again, and, next, still, besides, finally
Comparison	similarly, in the same way, likewise, also, again, once more
Contrasting	but, although, despite, however, instead, nevertheless, on the one hand... on the other hand, regardless, yet, in contrast.
Cause and Effect	because, consequently, thus, therefore, then, to this end, since, so, as a result, if... then, accordingly
Examples	for example, for instance, such as, to illustrate, indeed, in fact, specifically
Place	near, far, here, there, to the left/right, next to, above, below, beyond, opposite, beside
Repetition, Summary, or Conclusion	as mentioned earlier, as noted, in other words, in short, on the whole, to summarize, therefore, as a result, to conclude, in conclusion
Addition	and, also, furthermore, moreover

Review Video: Transition Words
Visit mometrix.com/academy and enter code: 707563

Conclusion

The conclusion of a composition should summarize the controlling idea and show that it has been explained well. A good conclusion shows the reader why the author's controlling idea is meaningful and important and how the supporting details should help the reader understand the controlling idea. The conclusion should also give the reader something to think about that is related to the controlling idea. For example, in the conclusion, the author can invite readers to think about how they feel or what they think after reading the composition. Some things to avoid when writing conclusions include:

- Introducing a completely new idea
- Apologizing for one's opinions or writing
- Repeating the controlling idea word for word rather than summarizing them
- Using the conclusion to summarize every detail in the composition

Review Video: Drafting Conclusions
Visit mometrix.com/academy and enter code: 209408

Chapter Quiz

1. "Too," "and," "next," "still," "besides," and "finally" are all what type of transitional word?

a. Time
b. Sequence
c. Comparison
d. Contrasting

2. Which of the following should be avoided in an essay conclusion?

a. Reminding the reader of the central idea by repeating it word for word
b. Showing the reader why the author's central idea is meaningful and important
c. Showing that the central idea has been explained well
d. Giving the reader something to think about that is related to the central idea

3. A helpful, informative paragraph will often have how many sentences?

a. One to three sentences
b. Three to five sentences
c. Five to ten sentences
d. Ten to fifteen sentences

4. The body of an essay should do all of the following, EXCEPT:

a. Introduce the central idea
b. Demonstrate the central idea
c. Explain the central idea
d. Give information about the central idea

Chapter Quiz Answer Key

1. B: See section **Types of Transitional Words**

2. A: See section **Conclusion**

3. B: See section **Length of a Paragraph**

4. A: See section **Body**

Grammar

Subjects and Predicates

Subjects

Every sentence needs a subject and a predicate. The **subject** of a sentence names who or what the sentence is about. The subject may be directly stated in a sentence, or the subject may be implied. The **complete subject** includes the simple subject and any **modifiers**, such as adjectives, articles, prepositions, and adverbs, that go with it. To find the complete subject, ask *Who* or *What* before the verb to complete the question. The answer, including any modifiers, is the complete subject. To find the **simple subject**, remove all of the modifiers in the complete subject.

Examples:

simple subject

The small, red car is the one that he wants for Christmas.

complete subject

simple subject

The young artist is coming over for dinner.

complete subject

Review Video: Subjects in English
Visit mometrix.com/academy and enter code: 444771

An imperative sentence is a sentence that gives someone instructions or makes a request to someone. In **imperative** sentences, the verb's subject is understood, but is not actually present in the sentence. For example, this about the sentence *Drive to the store*. This sentence is a command, and the subject is *you*. If the subject were directly stated, the sentence would be *You, drive to the store*. Another fact to consider is that, normally, the subject comes before the verb. However, the subject comes after the verb in sentences that begin with *There are* or *There was*.

Direct:

John knows the way to the park.	Who knows the way to the park?	John
The cookies need ten more minutes.	What needs ten minutes?	The cookies
By five o'clock, Bill will need to leave.	Who needs to leave?	Bill
There are five letters on the table for him.	What is on the table?	Five letters
There were coffee and doughnuts in the house.	What was in the house?	Coffee and doughnuts

Implied:

Go to the post office for me.	Who is going to the post office?	You
Come and sit with me, please?	Who needs to come and sit?	You

PREDICATES

In a sentence, there is always a predicate and a subject. The subject tells what the sentence is about, and the **predicate** explains or describes the subject.

Think about the sentence *He sings*. In this sentence, we have a subject, *He*, and a predicate, *sings*. This is all that is needed for a sentence to be complete. Most sentences contain more information, but if this is all the information that is given in a sentence, then it is a complete sentence.

Now, let's look at another sentence: *John and Jane sing on Tuesday nights at the dance hall.*

subject: John and Jane | predicate: sing on Tuesday nights at the dance hall.

John and Jane sing on Tuesday nights at the dance hall.

SUBJECT-VERB AGREEMENT

Verbs **agree** with their subjects in number. In other words, singular subjects need singular verbs. Plural subjects need plural verbs. **Singular** is for **one** person, place, or thing. **Plural** is for **more than one** person, place, or thing. Subjects and verbs must also share the same point of view, as in first, second, or third person.

Review Video: Subject-Verb Agreement
Visit mometrix.com/academy and enter code: 479190

NUMBER AGREEMENT EXAMPLES:

Single Subject and Verb: Dan (singular subject) calls (singular verb) home.

Dan is one person. So, the singular verb *calls* is needed.

Plural Subject and Verb: Dan and Bob (plural subject) call (plural verb) home.

More than one person needs the plural verb *call*.

PERSON AGREEMENT EXAMPLES:

First Person: I *am* walking.

Second Person: You *are* walking.

Third Person: He *is* walking.

COMPLICATIONS WITH SUBJECT-VERB AGREEMENT

WORDS BETWEEN SUBJECT AND VERB

Words that come between the simple subject and the verb do not affect subject-verb agreement.

Examples:

The joy (singular subject) of my life returns (singular verb) home tonight.

The phrase *of my life* does not affect the verb *returns.*

singular subject — singular verb

The question that still remains unanswered is "Who are you?"

Don't let the phrase "*that still remains…*" confuse you. The subject *question* goes with the verb *is.*

Compound Subjects

A compound subject is formed when two or more nouns joined by *and*, *or*, or *nor* act together as the subject of the sentence.

Joined by And

When a compound subject is joined by *and*, it is treated as a plural subject and requires a plural verb.

Examples:

plural subject — plural verb

You and Jon are invited to come to my house.

plural subject — plural verb

The pencil and paper belong to me.

Joined by Or/Nor

For a compound subject joined by *or* or *nor*, the verb must agree in number with the part of the subject that is closest to the verb.

Examples:

subject — verb

Today or tomorrow is the day.

subject — verb

Stan or Phil wants to read the book.

subject — verb

Neither the pen nor the book is on the desk.

subject — verb

Either the blanket or pillows arrive this afternoon.

Indefinite Pronouns as Subject

An indefinite pronoun is a pronoun that does not refer to a specific noun. Different indefinite pronouns are used as a singular noun, a plural noun, or change depending on how they are used.

Always Singular

Pronouns such as *each*, *either*, *everybody*, *anybody*, *somebody*, and *nobody* are always singular. This is because these pronouns always stand in for one person, place, or thing.

Examples:

singular subject: Each; singular verb: has

Each of the runners has a different bib number.

singular verb: Is; singular subject: either

Is either of you ready for the game?

Note: The words *each* and *either* can also be used as adjectives. For example, *each* person is unique. When one of these adjectives modifies the subject of a sentence, it is always a singular subject.

singular subject: Everybody; singular verb: grows

Everybody grows a day older every day.

singular subject: Anybody; singular verb: is

Anybody is welcome to bring a tent.

ALWAYS PLURAL

Pronouns such as *both*, *several*, and *many* are always plural. This is because these pronouns always stand in for more than one person, place, thing, or idea.

Examples:

plural subject: Both; plural verb: were

Both of the siblings were too tired to argue.

plural subject: Many; plural verb: have tried

Many have tried, but none have succeeded.

DEPEND ON CONTEXT

Pronouns such as *some*, *any*, *all*, *none*, *more*, and *most* can be either singular or plural depending on what they are representing in the context of the sentence.

Examples:

singular subject: All; singular verb: was

All of my dog's food was still there in his bowl.

plural subject: all; plural verb: were

By the end of the night, all of my guests were already excited about coming to my next party.

OTHER CASES INVOLVING PLURAL OR IRREGULAR FORM

Some nouns are **singular in meaning but plural in form**: news, mathematics, physics, and economics.

The *news is* coming on now.

Mathematics is my favorite class.

Some nouns are plural in form and meaning, and have **no singular equivalent**: scissors and pants.

> Do these *pants come* with a shirt?
>
> The *scissors are* for my project.

Note: Look to your **dictionary** for help when you aren't sure whether a noun with a plural form has a singular or plural meaning.

Example

Which word should go in the blank?

> Joan and Susan ____ going to the store this evening.

a. Is
b. Are
c. Am
d. Was

Try using each choice in the sentence. Choice A, *is*, forms this sentence: Joan and Susan is going to the store this evening. There are two people, Joan and Susan, who are going to the store. This makes the subject of the sentence plural. *Is* is a singular verb, meaning it does not agree with the subject and cannot be the answer.

Choice B, *are*, forms this sentence: Joan and Susan are going to the store this evening. The subject of the sentence is still plural. But *are* is a plural verb! The subject and verb agree, so *are* is the correct answer.

Choice C, *am*, forms this sentence: Joan and Susan am going to the store this evening. *Am* is a singular verb, and it is also only used in first person, when the writer or speaker is referring to themself. The subject is plural, and the sentence is in third person, so *am* is not the correct answer.

Choice D, *was*, forms this sentence: Joan and Susan was going to the store this evening. *Was* is a singular verb, so it does not agree with the plural subject in this sentence.

Complements

A complement is a noun, pronoun, or adjective that is used to give more information about the subject or verb in the sentence.

Direct Objects

A direct object is a noun or pronoun that takes or receives the **action** of a verb. A complete sentence does not need a direct object, so not all sentences will have them. When you are looking for a direct object, find the verb and ask *who* or *what.*

Examples:

> I took *the blanket.*
>
> Jane read *books.*

Indirect Objects

An indirect object is a word or group of words that show how an action had an **influence** on someone or something. If there is an indirect object in a sentence, then you always have a direct object in the sentence. When you are looking for the indirect object, find the verb and ask *to, for, whom*, or *what*.

Examples:

We taught [the old dog]₍indirect object₎ [a new trick]₍direct object₎.

I gave [them]₍indirect object₎ [a math lesson]₍direct object₎.

Review Video: Direct and Indirect Objects
Visit mometrix.com/academy and enter code: 817385

PHRASES

A phrase is a group of words that functions as a single part of speech, usually a noun, adjective, or adverb. A **phrase** is not a complete thought, and does not contain a subject, but it adds detail or explanation to a sentence, or renames something within the sentence.

CLAUSES

A clause is a group of words that contains both a subject and a predicate (verb). There are two types of clauses: independent and dependent. An **independent clause** contains a complete thought, while a **dependent (or subordinate) clause** does not. A dependent clause includes a subject and a verb, and may also contain additional information, but it cannot stand as a complete thought without being joined to an independent clause. Dependent clauses function within sentences as adjectives, adverbs, or nouns.

Example:

[I am running]₍independent clause₎ [because I want to stay in shape]₍dependent clause₎.

The clause *I am running* is an independent clause: it has a subject and a verb, and it gives a complete thought. The clause *because I want to stay in shape* is a dependent clause: it has a subject and a verb, but it does not express a complete thought. This is due to the fact that it begins with *because*, which shows that there is more information needed to complete the thought. This dependent clause adds detail to the independent clause to which it is attached.

Review Video: Independent and Dependent Clauses
Visit mometrix.com/academy and enter code: 556903

SENTENCE STRUCTURE

Sentence structure is based on the type and number of clauses in the sentence. Two common sentence structures are simple sentences and compound sentences:

SIMPLE

A simple sentence has one independent clause with no dependent clauses. A simple sentence may have a **compound subject** or a **compound verb**, or both.

Examples:

single subject | single verb
Judy watered the lawn.

compound subject | single verb
Judy and Alan watered the lawn.

single subject | compound verb | compound verb
Judy watered the lawn and pulled weeds.

compound subject | compound verb | compound verb
Judy and Alan watered the lawn and pulled weeds.

COMPOUND

A compound sentence has two or more independent clauses with no dependent clauses. Usually, the independent clauses are joined with a comma and a coordinating conjunction or with a semicolon.

Examples:

independent clause | independent clause
The time has come, and we are ready.

independent clause | independent clause
I woke up at dawn; the sun was just coming up.

COMPLEX

A complex sentence has one independent clause and at least one dependent clause.

Examples:

dependent clause | independent clause
Although he had the flu, Harry went to work.

independent clause | dependent clause
Marcia got married after she finished college.

Review Video: Sentence Structure
Visit mometrix.com/academy and enter code: 700478

SENTENCE FRAGMENTS

Recall that a group of words must contain at least one **independent clause** in order to be considered a sentence. If it doesn't contain even one independent clause, it is called a **sentence fragment**.

Choosing the best steps for **repairing** a sentence fragment depends on what type of fragment it is. If the fragment is a dependent clause, it can sometimes be fixed by simply removing a subordinating word, such as *when*, *because*, or *if*, from the beginning of the fragment. Alternatively, a dependent clause can be joined to a closely related neighboring sentence. If the fragment is missing some required part, like a subject or a verb, it may be fixed by simply adding the missing part.

Examples:

> **Fragment**: Because he wanted to sail the Mediterranean.
>
> **Removed subordinating word**: He wanted to sail the Mediterranean.
>
> **Combined with another sentence**: Because he wanted to sail the Mediterranean, he booked a Greek island cruise.

Example

Which of the following changes will NOT correct this sentence fragment?

Although she had found the coin first.

a. Remove *Although.*
b. Add a comma and *she let her brother keep it* after *first.*
c. Add *She let her brother keep the coin* before *although.*
d. Remove *first.*

Choice A suggests removing the word *although* to form the following sentence: She found the coin first. This option removes the subordinating conjunction to make the clause independent. The resulting sentence is complete, so removing *although* is an acceptable way to correct the fragment. Choice A is incorrect.

Choice B forms the following sentence: Although she had found the coin first, she let her brother keep it. A comma and an independent clause have been added to the sentence fragment to form a complex sentence. The resulting sentence is complete and written correctly, so choice B is incorrect.

Choice C forms the following sentence: She let her brother keep the coin although she had found the coin first. An independent clause has been added before the sentence fragment to form a complex sentence. This sentence is correctly written and complete, so choice C is an acceptable way to correct the fragment. Choice C is incorrect.

Choice D removes the word *first*, leaving *Although she had found the coin*. This is still a sentence fragment, since it is a single dependent clause. Choice D does not correct the fragment, so D is correct.

Run-on Sentences

Run-on sentences consist of multiple independent clauses that have not been joined together properly. Run-on sentences can be corrected in several different ways:

Join clauses properly: This can be done with a comma and coordinating conjunction, with a semicolon, or with a colon or dash if the second clause is explaining something in the first clause.

Example:

> **Incorrect**: I went on the trip, we visited lots of castles.
>
> **Corrected**: I went on the trip, and we visited lots of castles.

Split into separate sentences: This correction is best to use when the independent clauses are very long or when they are not closely related.

Example:

> **Incorrect**: The drive to New York takes ten hours, my uncle lives in Boston.
>
> **Corrected**: The drive to New York takes ten hours. My uncle lives in Boston.

Make one clause dependent: This is the easiest way to make the sentence correct and more interesting at the same time. It's often as simple as adding a subordinating word between the two clauses or before the first clause.

Example:

> **Incorrect**: I finally made it to the store and I bought some eggs.
>
> **Corrected**: When I finally made it to the store, I bought some eggs.

Reduce to one clause with a compound verb: If both clauses have the same subject, remove the subject from the second clause, and you now have just one clause with a compound verb.

Example:

> **Incorrect**: The drive to New York takes ten hours, it makes me very tired.
>
> **Corrected**: The drive to New York takes ten hours and makes me very tired.

Note: While these are the simplest ways to correct a run-on sentence, often the best way is to completely reorganize the thoughts in the sentence and rewrite it.

Comma Splices

A comma splice is a specific error that may appear in a run-on sentence. When a sentence has two independent clauses, but the clauses are joined with only a comma, a **comma splice** is formed. Remember that if two independent clauses are joined with a comma, a coordinating conjunction is also needed. Most of the solutions for fixing run-on sentences can also be used to correct a comma splice.

Example

> Rick wants to go see a movie tomorrow he would miss his sister's recital.

Identify the change that would NOT correct this run-on sentence.

a. Add a comma after *tomorrow*.
b. Split it into two sentences between *tomorrow* and *he*.
c. Add a comma and but after *tomorrow*.
d. Add a subordinating conjunction to make one of the clauses dependent.

Choice A says to add a comma after *tomorrow*. This forms the following sentence: Rick wants to go see a movie tomorrow, he would miss his sister's recital. A comma has been used to join two independent clauses, but there is no coordinating conjunction. This choice forms a comma splice, so it is not an acceptable correction for this sentence. Choice A is the correct answer.

Choice B says to split the sentence into two sentences. This forms the following two sentences: Rick wants to go see a movie tomorrow. He would miss his sister's recital. Both of these sentences are complete. This is an acceptable way to correct the run-on sentence, so choice B is incorrect.

Choice C says to add a coordinating conjunction after *tomorrow*. This forms the following sentence: Rick wants to go see a movie tomorrow, but he would miss his sister's recital. A comma and a coordinating conjunction have been added between the two independent clauses. This is an acceptable way to correct a run-on sentence. Choice C is incorrect.

Choice D says to add a subordinating conjunction to make one of the sentences dependent. There are many new sentences that could be created by adding a subordinating conjunction. For example, consider the following sentence: Although Rick wants to go see a movie tomorrow, he would miss his sister's recital. Alternatively, the following sentence could also be created: Rick wants to go see a movie tomorrow even though he would miss his sister's recital. Both of these sentences have an independent clause and a dependent clause. These sentences are both complete and written correctly, so choice D is incorrect.

EXAMPLE

Identify the sentence that has a comma splice.

a. Tom stopped at the store to buy supplies and his family met him at the campsite.
b. The ball rolled into the living room quietly, but it still startled the dog.
c. Theresa brought her mom some flowers, her mom did not have a vase.
d. Sweet potatoes, pecans, and brown sugar are all ingredients in my cousin's sweet potato casserole.

Choice A has two independent clauses joined by a coordinating conjunction. This is incorrect because there should be a comma before the coordinating conjunction. While the sentence is written incorrectly, there is no comma, so this sentence does not have a comma splice. Choice A is incorrect.

Choice B has two independent clauses joined by a comma and a coordinating conjunction. This is the correct way to write a compound sentence, so there is no error here. Choice B is incorrect.

Choice C has two independent clauses joined by a comma. This is incorrect because independent clauses should be joined together by a comma and a coordinating conjunction. When the comma is present without a coordinating conjunction between two independent clauses, a comma splice is formed. This means that choice C is correct.

Choice D is a simple sentence that contains one independent clause. The only commas used in this sentence are used to separate items in a list. There are no clauses that need to be joined or errors related to commas, so choice D does not contain a comma splice. Choice D is incorrect.

PARTS OF SPEECH

NOUNS

When you talk about a person, place, thing, or idea, you are talking about a **noun**. The two main types of nouns are **common** and **proper** nouns.

COMMON NOUNS

Common nouns are generic names for people, places, and things. Common nouns are not usually capitalized.

Examples of common nouns:

People: boy, girl, worker, manager

Places: school, bank, library, home

Things: dog, cat, truck, car

Proper Nouns

Proper nouns name specific people, places, or things. All proper nouns are capitalized.

Examples of proper nouns:

People: Abraham Lincoln, George Washington, Martin Luther King, Jr.

Places: Los Angeles, California; New York; Asia

Things: Statue of Liberty, Earth, Lincoln Memorial

Note: When referring to the planet that we live on, capitalize *Earth*. When referring to the dirt, rocks, or land, lowercase *earth*.

Singular and Plural Nouns

Singular nouns name **one** person, place, thing, or idea. **Plural nouns** name **more than one** person, place, thing, or idea. Most nouns have both a singular and plural form. Many plural nouns are spelled like the singular noun with an *-s* at the end, but this is not true for all plural nouns. Singular nouns that already end in an *s*, *o*, *ch*, *sh*, or *x* usually end in *-es* when they are in the plural form. Singular nouns that end in a consonant followed by the letter *y* will usually lose the *y* and end in *-ies* in the plural form, and words that end with the letter *f* or *fe* will usually lose the *f* and end in *-ves*.

Some plural nouns have much different spellings than their singular form, and some plural nouns are spelled the same as their singular form. There are more rules for spelling plural nouns, but these are the most common spelling changes.

Examples of singular nouns:

Typical nouns: dog, pencil, girl, store, hope, stingray

Nouns ending in *s*, *o*, *ch*, *sh*, or *x*: mass, hero, lunch, polish, fox

Nouns ending in a consonant and *y*: puppy, baby, fairy, sky

Nouns ending in *f* or *fe*: self, life, calf, hoof

Examples of plural nouns:

Typical nouns: dogs, pencils, girls, stores, hopes, stingrays

Nouns ending in *s*, *o*, *ch*, *sh*, or *x*: masses, heroes, lunches, polishes, foxes

Nouns ending in a consonant and *y*: puppies, babies, fairies, skies

Nouns ending in a vowel and *f* or *fe*: selves, lives, calves, hooves

Collective Nouns

Collective nouns are the names for a group of people, places, or things that function like singular nouns. The following are examples of collective nouns: *class, company, dozen, group, herd, team,* and *public*. Collective nouns usually require an article, such as *a*, *an*, and *the*, which shows that the noun is a single unit. For example, a choir is a group of singers. Even though there are many singers in a choir, the word choir describes a single group. If we refer to the members of the group, and not the group itself, it is no longer a collective noun.

> Incorrect: The *choir are* going to compete nationally this year.
>
> Correct: The *choir is* going to compete nationally this year.
>
> Incorrect: The *members* of the choir *is* competing nationally this year.
>
> Correct: The *members* of the choir *are* competing nationally this year.

Example

Find the error in the following sentence.

> John, Mary, and Claudia are all on the finance committee, which decide how the school's money is spent.

a. After *Claudia*, *are* should be changed to *is*.
b. After *money*, *is* should be changed to *are*.
c. After *which*, *decide* should be changed to *decides*.
d. The sentence is written correctly.

Choice A says that *are* should be changed to *is*. In this sentence, *are* is the verb that goes with the compound subject, John, Mary, and Claudia. Since the subject is plural, the verb that goes with it must also be plural. *Is* is a singular verb, so this would not be an appropriate change to make. Choice A is incorrect.

Choice B says that *is* should be changed to *are*. In the original sentence, the verb *is* refers to the noun *money*. Even though *money* may refer to more than one unit of currency, it is a collective noun, so it acts as a singular noun. *Are* is a plural verb, so it should not accompany the singular noun *money*. Choice B is incorrect.

Choice C says *decide* should be changed to *decides*. In the present tense, *decide* is used with plural nouns. *Decide* refers to *committee* in this sentence. A committee is a group of multiple people, but it functions as a singular noun because it is a collective noun. This means that *decide* should not go with *committee* and should be replaced with *decides*. Choice C is correct!

Choice D says that this sentence has no errors. In this sentence, the verb *decide* is used to refer to the collective noun *committee*. Since *decide* functions like a plural verb in this sentence, it cannot go with a collective noun. This is an error in the sentence, so choice D is incorrect.

Pronouns

Pronouns are words that are used to stand in for nouns. There are several different types of pronouns, but the two main types are subjective and objective pronouns. **Subjective** nouns and pronouns that those that are the subject of a sentence. **Objective** nouns and pronouns are those that are an object in a sentence. Another important type of pronoun is the personal pronoun, which refers to people. Personal pronouns can be subjective or objective. **Possessive** nouns and pronouns show possession or ownership. Pronouns can also be singular or plural.

Singular

Subjective	Objective	Possessive
I	Me	My, Mine
You	You	Your, Yours
He	Him	His
She	Her	Her, hers
It	It	Its
Who	Whom	Whose

Plural

Subjective	Objective	Possessive
we	us	our, ours
you	you	your, yours
they	them	their, theirs

Reflexive: Reflexive pronouns are pronouns that function as the object of a sentence and refer to the subject. Examples of reflexive pronouns include *myself, yourself, himself, herself, itself, ourselves, yourselves*, and *themselves.*

Indefinite: Indefinite pronouns are used to refer to multiple nouns or an undefined noun. Examples of indefinite nouns include *all, any, each, everyone, either/neither, one, some*, and *several.*

Review Video: Nouns and Pronouns
Visit mometrix.com/academy and enter code: 312073

EXAMPLE

Everyone felt better about themselves after his encouraging speech.

Which type of pronoun is NOT used in the sentence above?

a. Personal
b. Reflexive
c. Indefinite
d. Possessive

Choice A says that there is a personal pronoun in this sentence. Remember that personal pronouns are pronouns that replace a specific person's name or a group of people's names in a sentence. Also, they are either subjective or objective pronouns. In this sentence, *everyone* is the subject that acts on the object *themselves.* Neither of these pronouns take the place of a specific person's name, so there are no personal pronouns in the sentence. Choice A is correct!

Choice B says that there are no reflexive pronouns in this sentence. Remember that a reflexive pronoun is one that mentions the subject as the object of the sentence. In this sentence, the subject is *everyone* and the object is *themselves. Themselves* is used to refer to *everyone*, so *themselves* functions as a reflexive pronoun. Choice B is incorrect.

Choice C says that there are no indefinite pronouns in this sentence. Indefinite pronouns are used to represent a person, group, or thing that is not specified. In this sentence, the pronoun *everyone* is used. *Everyone* refers to a group of people, but does not specify which people. *Everyone* is an indefinite pronoun, so choice C is incorrect.

Choice D says that there are no possessive pronouns in this sentence. Remember that possessive pronouns are used to replace the name of a person or an object that possesses something. In this sentence, the encouraging speech is *his* speech. The speech belongs to *him*, so *his* is a possessive pronoun. Choice D is incorrect.

VERBS

If you want to write a sentence, then you need a verb. Without a verb, you have no sentence. The verb of a sentence indicates action or being. In other words, the verb shows something's action or state of being or the action that has been done to something.

ACTION VERBS AND LINKING VERBS

Action verbs show what the subject is doing. In other words, an action verb shows action. **Linking verbs** link the subject of a sentence to a noun or pronoun. They can also link a subject to an adjective, so the linking verb helps create a description. You always need a verb if you want a complete sentence. However, linking verbs on their own cannot be a complete sentence. Any verb that shows a condition and connects to a noun, pronoun, or adjective that describes the subject of a sentence is a linking verb.

Action: He sings. | Run! | Go! | I talk with him every day. | She reads.

Linking:

Incorrect: I am.

Correct: I am John. | The roses smell lovely. | I feel tired.

Review Video: Action Verbs and Linking Verbs
Visit mometrix.com/academy and enter code: 743142

VERB TENSES

A verb **tense** shows the different form of a verb to point to the time of an action. The present and past tense are indicated by the verb's form. An action in the present, *I talk,* can change form for the past: *I talked*. However, for future tense, an auxiliary, or helping, verb is sometimes needed to show the change in form.

Present: I talk
Past: I talked
Future: I will talk

Present: The action happens at the current time.

Example: He *walks* to the store every morning.

Past: The action happened in the past.

Example: He *walked* to the store an hour ago.

Future: The action is going to happen later.

Example: I *will walk* to the store tomorrow.

Irregular Verbs

While most verbs gain the suffix -ed when used in the past tense, irregular verbs receive different spelling changes when they are written in the past tense. For example, *walk* is a regular verb, and it becomes *walked* when written in the past tense. However, *run* is an irregular verb because it becomes *ran* when written in the past tense.

Example

Which of the following words is a regular verb?

a. Run
b. Warn
c. Hold
d. Catch

Remember that regular verbs are verbs that end in *-ed* when they are written in the past tense. Irregular verbs are spelled differently in past tense.

Choice A says that *run* is a regular verb. What is the past tense of *run*? Is it *runned* or *ran*? The past tense of *run* is *ran*, so it is an irregular verb. Choice A is incorrect.

Choice B says that *warn* is a regular verb. The past tense of *warn* is *warned*, which means that *warned* is a regular verb Choice B is correct.

Choice C says that *hold* is a regular verb. What is the past tense of *hold*? Is it *holded* or *held*? The past tense of *hold* is *held*, so it is an irregular verb. Choice C is incorrect.

Choice D says that *catch* is a regular verb. What is the past tense of *catch*? Is it *catched* or *caught*? The past tense of *catch* is *caught*, so it is an irregular verb. Choice D is incorrect.

Adjectives

An **adjective** is a word that is used to modify a noun or pronoun. An adjective answers a question: *Which one? What kind?* or *How many?* Usually, adjectives come before the words that they modify, but they may also come after a linking verb.

> Which one? The *third* suit is my favorite.
>
> What kind? This suit is *navy blue.*
>
> How many? I am going to buy *four* pairs of socks to match the suit.

Review Video: Descriptive Text
Visit mometrix.com/academy and enter code: 174903

Comparison with Adjectives

Some adjectives are relative, and other adjectives are absolute. Adjectives that are **relative** can show the comparison between things. **Absolute** adjectives can also show comparison, but they do so in a different way. Let's say that you are reading two books. You think that one book is perfect, and the other book is not exactly perfect. It is not possible for one book to be more perfect than the other. Either you think that the book is perfect, or you think that the book is imperfect. In this case, perfect and imperfect are absolute adjectives.

Relative adjectives will show the different **degrees** of something or someone to something else or someone else. The three degrees of adjectives include positive, comparative, and superlative.

The **positive** degree is the normal form of an adjective.

Example: This work is *difficult*. | She is *smart*.

The **comparative** degree compares one person or thing to another person or thing.

Example: This work is *more difficult* than your work. | She is *smarter* than me.

The **superlative** degree compares more than two people or things.

Example: This is the *most difficult* work of my life. | She is the *smartest* lady in school.

Review Video: Adjectives
Visit mometrix.com/academy and enter code: 470154

EXAMPLE

What type of adjective is used in the following sentence?

The day John got married was the happiest day of his life.

a. Absolute
b. Comparative
c. Positive
d. Superlative

First find the adjective. The noun that is being described is *day*, so the adjective is *happiest*. Remember the difference between the different types of adjectives. Can one day be happier than another? How many days are being compared?

Choice A says *happiest* is an absolute adjective. Absolute adjectives cannot have different degrees. This sentence says that it was the happiest day of John's life, which means that it was happier than other days in his life. This means that *happiest* cannot be an absolute adjective, so A is incorrect.

Choice B says *happiest* is a comparative adjective. Comparative adjectives are used to compare two nouns. If John's wedding day is the happiest day of his life, then that day is being compared to thousands of other days. Also, *happiest* has the suffix *-est*, which is used in superlative adjectives that compare more than two nouns. These two facts show that *happiest* is not a comparative noun, so B is incorrect.

Choice C says that *happiest* is a positive adjective. Positive adjectives are the types of adjectives that simply describe nouns, but can be changed to either the comparative or superlative form. *Happy* is a positive noun because it can be used to describe a noun, but it can also be changed to *happier* or *happiest* in order to compare things. Since *happy* is a positive adjective that can be changed to *happiest* when more than two happy things are being compared, *happiest* is not a positive adjective. C is incorrect.

Choice D says that *happiest* is a superlative adjective. Superlative adjectives are used to compare three or more nouns. Since each of the thousands of days in John's life are being compared, it is true that more than three nouns are being compared. Again, the suffix *-est* is also used, which shows that this adjective is superlative. D is correct!

EXAMPLE

Choose the word, or words, that best completes the sentence.

Marie's meeting was ____ than Dana's meeting.

a. The most boring
b. More boring
c. Boring
d. Bored

Choice A says that *the most boring* best completes the sentence. In the sentence, one meeting is being compared to another, so only two meetings are being compared. Since choice A uses the word *most*, this choice is a superlative adjective. Superlative adjectives are used to compare three or more nouns, not two. Choice A is incorrect.

Choice B says that *more boring* best completes the sentence. This choice uses the word *more*, instead of *most*. *More* is used in comparative adjectives to compare two nouns. Since two meetings are being compared in the sentence, the comparative adjective *more boring* is the best choice. B is correct.

Choice C says that *boring* best completes the sentence. The only word in this answer choice is *boring*, which is a positive adjective used to describe a noun. While the sentence suggests that both meetings were boring, the sentence is comparing the two meetings. Positive adjectives are used to describe, not compare, so choice C is incorrect.

Choice D says that *bored* best completes the sentence. Like choice C, *bored* is a positive adjective used to describe a noun. Since positive adjectives without words like *more* or *most* or suffixes like -*er* or -*est* are not used to compare, *bored* is not a good choice for this sentence. *Bored* is also used to describe a state or emotion, so it is not logical to describe a meeting as bored in this sentence. D is incorrect.

ADVERBS

An **adverb** is a word that is used to **modify,** or describe, a verb, adjective, or another adverb. Usually, adverbs answer one of these questions: *When? Where? How?* and *Why?* The negatives *not* and *never* are considered adverbs. Adverbs that modify adjectives or other adverbs **strengthen** or **weaken** the words that they modify.

Examples:

He walks *quickly* through the crowd.

The water flows *smoothly* on the rocks.

Note: Adverbs are usually indicated by the suffix -*ly*, which has been added to the root word. For instance, *quick* can be made into an adverb by adding -*ly* to construct *quickly*. Some words that end in -*ly* do not follow this rule and can function as other parts of speech. Examples of adjectives ending in -*ly* include: *early, friendly, holy, lonely, silly*, and *ugly*. To know if a word that ends in -*ly* is an adjective or adverb, check your dictionary. Also, while many adverbs end in -*ly*, you need to remember that not all adverbs end in -*ly*.

Examples:

He is *never* angry.

You are *too* irresponsible to travel alone.

Types of Adverbs

Different types of adverbs are used to describe particular aspects of a verb, adjective, or other adverb. The following are examples of common types of adverbs:

Time: Some adverbs show when something was done, such as *yesterday*, *today*, or *in two days.*

Manner: Some adverbs show the way something was done, such as *hurriedly*, *neatly*, *grumpily*, or *loudly.*

Frequency: Some adverbs show how often something was done, such as *seldom*, *often*, *never*, or *often.*

Degree: Some adverbs show how much or to what degree something was done, such as *completely*, *barely*, *highly*, or *halfway.*

Conjunctive: Conjunctive adverbs are used similarly to conjunctions, as they connect different ideas, but they can connect ideas from different clauses or sentences. Some examples of conjunctive adverbs are *however*, *alternatively*, *likewise*, and *then.*

Comparison with Adverbs

The rules for comparing adverbs are the same as the rules for adjectives.

The **positive** degree is the standard form of an adverb.

Example: He arrives *soon.* | She speaks *softly* to her friends.

The **comparative** degree compares one person or thing to another person or thing.

Example: He arrives *sooner* than Sarah. | She speaks *more softly* than him.

The **superlative** degree compares more than two people or things.

Example: He arrives *soonest* of the group. | She speaks the *most softly* of any of her friends.

Review Video: Adverbs
Visit mometrix.com/academy and enter code: 713951

Example

Identify the conjunctive adverb in the following sentences.

Every night, Savannah's brother loudly gets up to get a glass of water. Consequently, she has started sleeping with earmuffs on so that he does not wake her up at night.

a. Every night
b. Loudly
c. Consequently
d. At night

Choice A says that *every night* is a conjunctive adverb. What does *every night* describe in this sentence? It describes how often Savannah's brother loudly gets a glass of water. This means that *every night* shows the frequency that Savannah's brother does this action. Since *every night* is an adverb that shows frequency, choice A is incorrect.

Choice B says that *loudly* is a conjunctive adverb. In this sentence, what does *loudly* describe? It describes the way that Savannah's brother gets a glass of water each night. This means that *loudly* is an adverb that shows manner. *Loudly* is not a conjunctive adverb, so choice B is incorrect.

Choice C says that *consequently* is a conjunctive adverb. What function does *consequently* have in this sentence? It shows the reason that Savannah started wearing earmuffs while she sleeps. It also shows a connection between the information in the first sentence and the information in the second sentence. Since *consequently* connects the ideas in these sentences, it is a conjunctive adverb. Choice C is correct.

Choice D says that *at night* is a conjunctive adverb. *At* and *night* work together to form an adverbial phrase. Which type of adverb do they form? In this sentence, *at night* shows when Savannah wants to avoid being woken up by her brother. This makes *at night* an adverb that shows time, meaning that *at night* is not a conjunctive adverb and choice D is incorrect.

PREPOSITIONS

A **preposition** is a word placed before a noun or pronoun that shows the relationship between an object and another word in the sentence.

Common prepositions:

about	before	during	on	under
after	beneath	for	over	until
against	between	from	past	up
among	beyond	in	through	with
around	by	of	to	within
at	down	off	toward	without

Examples:

> The napkin is *in* the drawer.
>
> The Earth rotates *around* the Sun.
>
> The needle is *beneath* the haystack.
>
> Can you find "me" *among* the words?

PREPOSITIONAL PHRASES

One important thing to know about prepositions is that they form special phrases, called prepositional phrases. A **prepositional phrase** begins with a preposition and ends with a noun or pronoun that is the object of the preposition. Normally, the prepositional phrase functions as an **adjective** or an **adverb** within the sentence.

Examples:

The picnic is on the blanket. (prepositional phrase: "on the blanket")

I am sick with a fever today. (prepositional phrase: "with a fever")

Among the many flowers, John found a four-leaf clover. (prepositional phrase: "Among the many flowers,")

Be careful not to mistake the object in a prepositional phrase as the subject of a sentence. The subject of the sentence will not be found in a prepositional phrase because a prepositional phrase is used to describe how an object is related to the subject. Prepositional phrases do not influence subject-verb agreement.

Prepositional phrases do not influence subject-verb agreement. For example, consider the following sentence:

The basket of clothes is on the floor in the laundry room. (simple subject: "basket"; prepositional phrase: "of clothes"; verb: "is")

This sentence contains a prepositional phrase between the simple subject and the verb. The simple subject is *basket*, which is a singular noun, and the verb is *is*, which is a singular verb. They are separated by the prepositional phrase "of clothes." Even though the plural noun *clothes* comes right before the singular verb *is*, this verb shows the action of the singular noun *basket*.

Review Video: Prepositions
Visit mometrix.com/academy and enter code: 946763

EXAMPLE

Which of the following could NOT complete the sentence?

She went ____ the cave.

a. Sadly
b. Into
c. From
d. Through

Choice A says that the missing word is *sadly*. The blank is between *went* and *the cave*, meaning that the missing word will connect these pieces of the sentence. While *sadly* could be used here to show how the girl felt, there would still be missing information. A preposition is needed here to show whether she entered, exited, or stood outside of the cave. *Sadly* is an adverb, so A is the correct answer.

Choice B says that *into* would complete the sentence. Does *into* complete the sentence without leaving missing information? To say *she went into the cave* is a logical, complete sentence. Choice B is incorrect.

Choice C says that the missing word is *from*. This creates the sentence *she went from the cave*. Since she could have left the cave to go somewhere else, this is also a logical, complete sentence. Choice C is incorrect.

Choice D says that *through* would complete the sentence. The sentence would read *she went through the cave*. Since she could have explored the whole cave or found an exit on the other side of it, *through* can logically complete the sentence. Choice D is incorrect.

EXAMPLE

Identify the prepositional phrase in the following sentence.

Mable visited the store to buy some vegetables.

a. To buy
b. Visited the store
c. The store to buy
d. To buy some vegetables

Remember the pieces of a prepositional phrase. Prepositional phrases should begin with a preposition and end with a noun or pronoun. Considering these rules, can any of the answer choices be eliminated? Choice B and choice C can be eliminated because neither choice begins with a preposition!

That leaves choices A and D. Choice A says that the prepositional phrase is *to buy*. This does start with a preposition, and it does give more information about Mable's trip to the store. However, it does not end with a noun or pronoun. Choice D says that the prepositional phrase is *to buy some vegetables*. Choice D begins with a preposition and ends with a noun, and it explains why Mabel went to the store.

Choice D is the only choice that has all of the pieces of a prepositional phrase, so D is correct!

EXAMPLE

Read the sentence below and answer the following question.

A band with 15 members _____ performing at my restaurant tonight.

Identify the verb that best completes the sentence.

a. Were
b. Is
c. Are
d. Are not

This question is asking which verb should go in the blank. There are a couple of reasons why choosing the correct verb for this sentence may be confusing. First of all, there are two nouns that appear before the verb. Second, one of these nouns is singular and one is plural.

The first step is to determine which noun goes with the verb. The two nouns are *band* and *members*. While *members* is closest to the blank, it is part of a prepositional phrase that describes *band*. The subject of the sentence is *band*, so the verb must agree with *band*.

Is *band* singular or plural? The sentence says that the band has multiple members, but there is only one band. *Band* is a collective noun, meaning that it is a singular noun. This means that the correct verb will also be singular. With this in mind, can any of the answer choices be eliminated?

Choices A, C, and D are all plural verbs. Even though the blank appears after a plural noun, this noun is part of a prepositional phrase. The verb should match the singular subject *band*. The only choice with a singular verb is choice B, so B is the correct answer.

CONJUNCTIONS

Conjunctions join words, phrases, or clauses and they show the connection between the joined pieces. **Coordinating conjunctions** connect equal parts of sentences. Coordinating conjunctions can also be used to create compound subjects and compound predicates, in addition to compound sentences.

COORDINATING CONJUNCTIONS

The **coordinating conjunctions** include: *and, but, yet, or, nor, for,* and *so*

Compound Subjects:

compound subject

Terry *and* Marissa went to the movies last Saturday.

compund subject

Either pumpkin pie *or* apple pie would be a good dessert to bring to Thanksgiving dinner.

compound subject

Neither the clownfish *nor* the goldfish liked the new fish food very much.

Compound Predicates:

compound predicate

Veronica left school *and* picked up her sister from soccer practice.

compound predicate

The cat did not take a nap *or* play with the dog yesterday.

Compound Sentences:

The rock was small, *but* it was heavy.

She drove in the night, *and* he drove in the day.

Bill dressed nicely today, *for* he must give an important presentation this afternoon.

SUBORDINATING CONJUNCTIONS

Subordinating conjunctions link dependent clauses, clauses with either a subject or a predicate, to independent clauses, clauses with both a subject and a predicate, to form a complex sentence. The subordinating conjunction will always be at the beginning of the dependent clause. When the dependent clause is at the beginning of the sentence, it will end with a comma. When the independent clause is at the beginning of the sentence, no comma is needed.

Common **subordinating conjunctions** include:

after	since	whenever
although	so that	where
because	unless	wherever
before	until	whether
in order that	when	while

Examples:

I am hungry *because* I did not eat breakfast.

He went home *when* everyone left.

While her brother ate dinner, she played his favorite video game.

Review Video: Subordinating Conjunctions
Visit mometrix.com/academy and enter code: 958913

Example

Which of the following is a complex sentence?

a. Joseph went grocery shopping and put all of the groceries away at home.
b. Joseph went grocery shopping, and he put all of the groceries away at home.
c. Joseph went grocery shopping and put all of the groceries away when he got home.
d. Joseph went grocery shopping; he put all of the groceries away at home.

Choice A contains one subject and a compound predicate. Because there is only one subject, Joseph, there is only one clause. Since the sentence is made of one independent clause and a prepositional phrase, it is a simple sentence, and choice A is incorrect.

Choice B contains two clauses. The clauses are separated by a comma and a coordinating conjunction, and both are independent clauses. This sentence contains a prepositional phrase and two independent clauses, so it is a compound sentence. Choice B is incorrect.

Choice C contains two clauses. There are two subjects in the sentence, *Joseph* and *he*. Even though one clause is much shorter than the other, these subjects each go with a different clause. The first clause is independent. The second clause is dependent, as it begins with the word *when*. Since the sentence is made of one independent clause and one dependent clause, it is a complex sentence. Choice C is correct.

Choice D contains two clauses. They are both independent clauses, because they both contain a subject and a predicate, and they both form complete thoughts. Since there is no coordinating conjunction, they are linked by a semicolon. Since the sentence is made from two independent clauses, it is a compound sentence. Choice D is incorrect.

End Punctuation

Periods

Use a period to end all sentences except direct questions and exclamations. Periods are also used for abbreviations.

Examples: 3 p.m. | 2 a.m. | Mr. Jones | Mrs. Stevens | Dr. Smith | Bill, Jr. | Pennsylvania Ave.

Note: An abbreviation is a shortened form of a word or phrase.

Question Marks

Question marks should be used following a **direct question**. A polite request can be followed by a period instead of a question mark.

Direct Question: What is for lunch today? | How are you? | Why is that the answer?

Polite Requests: Can you please send me the item tomorrow. | Will you please walk with me on the track.

Review Video: Question Marks
Visit mometrix.com/academy and enter code: 118471

Exclamation Marks

Exclamation marks are used after a word group or sentence that shows much feeling or has special importance. Exclamation marks should not be overused. They are saved for proper **exclamatory interjections**.

Example: We're going to the finals! | You have a beautiful car! | "That's crazy!" she yelled.

Review Video: Exclamation Points
Visit mometrix.com/academy and enter code: 199367

Commas

The comma is a punctuation mark that can help you understand connections in a sentence. Not every sentence needs a comma. However, if a sentence needs a comma, you need to put it in the right place. A comma in the wrong place or a missing comma will make a sentence's meaning unclear. These are some of the rules for commas:

Use Case	Example
Before a **coordinating conjunction** joining independent clauses in **compound sentences**	Bob caught three fish, and I caught two fish.
Between **items in a series**	I will bring the turkey, the pie, and the coffee.
After a **dependent clause** that **begins a complex sentence**	Before she left, Ashley turned off all of the lights in her house.
After **transition words**	Consequently, Joel's mother grounded him.
After a **prepositional phrase** at the **beginning of a sentence**	At 10 in the evening, Georgia finally arrived home from work.

Review Video: When to Use a Comma
Visit mometrix.com/academy and enter code: 786797

EXAMPLE

Identify the sentence that contains an error.

a. While my brother did the dishes I folded the laundry.
b. My brother did the dishes, and I folded the laundry at the same time.
c. I folded the laundry while my brother did the dishes.
d. My brother and I worked on our chores at the same time.

Look over the answer choices. Remember that a sentence's structure depends on the types of clauses in the sentence. Sometimes, punctuation marks are required to properly link clauses, such as when linking a dependent clause followed by an independent clause or linking two independent clauses separated by a coordinating conjunction.

Choice A is a complex sentence, since it contains a dependent clause and an independent clause. Remember that when a dependent clause comes before an independent clause, a comma should follow the dependent clause. When an independent clause comes before a dependent clause, the comma is not needed. In this sentence, which type of clause comes first? The dependent clause comes first, so there is a comma missing in this sentence. This sentence does contain an error, so choice A is correct.

Which type of sentence is choice B? It is a compound sentence because it is made of two independent clauses. These clauses are joined by a comma and a coordinating conjunction. Remember that if a coordinating conjunction is used to join two independent clauses, a comma must be used immediately after the first clause. Leaving out the comma results in a run-on sentence, and using a comma to join independent clauses without a coordinating conjunction creates a comma splice. The sentence does not contain an error, so choice B is incorrect.

Choice C is another complex sentence. It contains an independent clause followed by a dependent clause. Even though the dependent clause begins with *while*, no comma is needed because the independent clause comes before the dependent clause. This sentence does not contain an error, so choice C is incorrect.

Which type of sentence is choice D? It is a simple sentence because it is made of one independent clause. There are no clauses that need to be connected using conjunctions or commas, so this sentence does not contain an error. Choice D is incorrect.

QUOTATION MARKS

Use quotation marks to close off **direct quotations** of a person's written or spoken words, which are also called **dialogue**. Do not use quotation marks around indirect quotations. An indirect quotation gives someone's message without using the person's exact words. Use **single quotation marks** to close off a quotation inside a quotation.

> **Direct Quote**: Nancy said, "I am waiting for Henry to arrive."
>
> **Indirect Quote**: Henry said that he is going to be late to the meeting.
>
> **Quote inside a Quote**: The teacher asked, "Has everyone read Martin Luther King's 'I Have a Dream' speech?"

Quotation marks should be used around the titles of **short works**: newspaper and magazine articles, poems, short stories, songs, television episodes, and radio programs. Titles of **long works** should be italicized when they are part of a typed composition or underlined when they are part of a handwritten composition.

Examples:

"Rip Van Winkle" (short story by Washington Irving)

"O Captain! My Captain!" (poem by Walt Whitman)

Review Video: Quotation Marks
Visit mometrix.com/academy and enter code: 884918

EXAMPLE

Identify the correct place for the first quotation mark in the following sentence.

After her brother threw a baseball inside, Hallie said, If you ever do that again, I'll tell mom" and took the ball.

a. Before *Hallie*
b. Before *said*
c. Before *if*
d. Before *threw*

Remember that quotation marks are used to identify the words that someone wrote or said. This means that the correct place for quotation marks to go is around the words that were spoken aloud or written. This question asks where the quotation marks should start, which means that the answer will include the first word of dialogue. Consider this as you read each answer choice.

Choice A says the quotation marks should start before *Hallie*. Is *Hallie* the first word of dialogue? No, Hallie is the person saying the dialogue. The words *Hallie said* form the dialogue tag, which tells who said the dialogue and how they said it. Quotes do not include dialogue tags, so dialogue tags should not be inside of quotation marks. Choice A is incorrect.

Choice B says the quotation marks should start before *said*. The word *said* is also part of the dialogue tag. The dialogue tag should go right before the first quotation mark or right after the last one, but it should not be within the quotation marks. Choice B is incorrect.

Choice C says the quotation marks should start before *if*. In this sentence, *if* is the first word spoken by Hallie, which makes it the first word of dialogue. Remember that the first quotation mark should go right before the first word of the quote. This means that choice C is correct!

Choice D says the quotation marks should start before *threw*. *Threw* is not part of the quotation, so it is certainly not the first word of dialogue. Choice D is incorrect.

EXAMPLE

Choose the sentence that contains a correctly punctuated title.

a. Edgar Allan Poe wrote many poems and short stories, such as *The Raven* and *The Black Cat*.
b. *Great Expectations* is her favorite novel.
c. I think "Romeo and Juliet" is William Shakespeare's most well-known play.
d. "The Great Gatsby" is a novel that has been made into multiple movies.

Choice A contains two titles in italics. Titles of long, or major, works should be italicized. This sentence includes the title of a poem and a short story. Both of these are short, or minor, works, so they should be in quotation marks rather than italics. Choice A is incorrect.

Choice B contains one title in italics. Remember that italics are for major works. The title in this sentence is the title of a novel, which is a major work. The title in this sentence is appropriately punctuated, so choice B is correct.

Choice C contains a title in quotation marks. Quotation marks should be used for titles of short, or minor, works. This sentence includes the title of a play. Plays are considered major works, so this title should be italicized. Choice C is incorrect.

Choice D contains one title in quotation marks. This is the title of a novel, so it is the title of a major work. The title should be italicized, but it is in quotation marks. Choice D is incorrect.

APOSTROPHES

An apostrophe is used to show **possession** or the **deletion of letters in contractions**. An apostrophe is not needed with the possessive pronouns *his, hers, its, ours, theirs, whose*, and *yours*.

Singular Nouns: David's car | a book's theme | my brother's board game

Plural Nouns that end with -*s*: the scissors' handle | boys' basketball

Plural Nouns that end without -*s*: Men's department | the people's adventure

Review Video: Apostrophes
Visit mometrix.com/academy and enter code: 213068

Review Video: Punctuation Errors in Possessive Pronouns
Visit mometrix.com/academy and enter code: 221438

APOSTROPHES IN CONTRACTIONS

Contractions are combinations of words. Contractions involve taking two words, removing at least one letter from one of the words, putting an apostrophe in its place, and removing the space. For example, *does not* can be written as the contraction *doesn't*. The *o* is removed from *not* and is replaced with an apostrophe, which represents the removed letter, so it appears as *n't*. The space after does is then removed, turning *does not* into the contraction *doesn't*. Some more examples of contractions are listed below.

First Word	Second Word	Contraction
Can	Not	Can't
Do	Not	Don't
She	Will	She'll
They	Will	They'll
He	Is	He's
It	Is	It's
They	Are	They're

First Word	Second Word	Contraction
I	Am	I'm

Not all words can be used to form contractions, but many small, commonly used words can.

CAPITALIZATION

One important part of using correct grammar is properly capitalizing words. Usually, only nouns will be capitalized, but there are some exceptions. The most important capitalization rule is that the first word of every sentence, no matter what part of speech it is, should be capitalized. Another exception is that the pronoun *I* should always be capitalized.

Proper nouns are always capitalized, but sometimes it can be tricky to decide whether or not a noun is a proper noun. Some words that are usually common nouns may become proper nouns when used with other words or phrases. Also, when words that are not nouns are used with a noun, or when a group of words are used together as one noun, those words may also need to be capitalized.

TITLES OF BOOKS, STORIES, AND ESSAYS

Most of the words in titles of things like books, stories, and essays should be capitalized, but some should not. The very first word in a title should always be capitalized. Any other word in a title that is a noun, pronoun, adjective, verb or adverb should be capitalized. Articles, such as *a* or *the*, should not be capitalized. Short conjunctions and prepositions are usually not capitalized.

ABBREVIATIONS, INITIALS, AND ACRONYMS

Abbreviations are shortened versions of other words. When an abbreviation shortens, or abbreviates, a word that should be capitalized, the abbreviation's first letter should also be capitalized. When the shortened word is a noun that is not capitalized, the abbreviation should be in lowercase. Initials are usually written using the first letter from multiple words. For example, John Fitzgerald Kennedy is commonly referred to by his initials, JFK. Acronyms also use the first letter from multiple words, but they are different from initials because they form words on their own. For example, NASA is an acronym for National Aeronautics and Space Administration. Some acronyms, like NASA, omit small words, such as *and*, *of*, and *for*. When initials and acronyms are used for proper nouns, each letter should be capitalized.

The types of words and phrases in the chart below are proper nouns and should always be capitalized:

	Description	Example
Historical Periods	A range of time in history that is related to specific events or circumstances	During the Romantic Period, many authors and poets wrote about their emotions.
Historical Events	Names of important events that happened in history	Napoleon Bonaparte led France after the French Revolution.
Historical Documents	Titles of important papers or compositions that are connected to historical events	The Mayflower Compact was written to create rules and expectations for the colony in Plymouth.

	Description	Example
Languages	Names of the different languages that people speak	I want to learn to speak Cantonese, Spanish, and German.
Races and Ethnicities	Words often used to describe a person's heritage or cultural group	Malia taught her granddaughter how to hula so she could share a tradition of her Native Hawaiian heritage with her.
Nationalities	Words that describe which country a person is from	My teacher who moved to Canada last year is Romanian.
Organizations	Titles of official groups formed by people	Fewer than half of the states in America have a team in the National Basketball Association.

Review Video: Capitalization in Grammar
Visit mometrix.com/academy and enter code: 369678

Example

Identify the capitalization mistake in the following sentences.

> My brother and I want to open a bakery, so we discussed what we should call it. I wanted to give it a name that would form the acronym Bake, but we couldn't think of a good name using those letters. My brother suggested Bakery Brothers and said that if we ever need to abbreviate the name, we can call it Bakery Bros. or BB.

a. All of the letters in *Bake* should be capitalized.
b. *Bakery Brothers* should be in lowercase.
c. All of the letters in *Bros.* should be capitalized.
d. The second *B* in *BB* should be lowercase.

There are three types of abbreviations in these sentences. The second sentence contains an acronym, and the third sentence contains a shortened word and an initialism. Consider the different capitalization rules for each of these to identify the error in the sentences.

Choice A says that all of the letters in *Bake* should be capitalized. Even though *bake* is a verb that usually should not be capitalized at all, it is used as an acronym in this sentence. That means that each letter should be capitalized, so choice A is correct.

Choice B says that all of the letters in *Bakery Brothers* should be in lowercase. In the sentences, *Bakery Brothers* is the full name of the bakery. Since it is the name of a place, *Bakery Brothers* is a proper noun. It is correctly capitalized, so choice B is incorrect.

Choice C says that all of the letters in *Bros.* should be capitalized. *Bros.* is a shortening of *brothers.* Remember that shortened words should follow the same capitalization rules as the original word. Since the first letter of *brothers* is capitalized in the phrase *Bakery Brothers*, *Bros.* is written correctly. Choice C is incorrect.

Choice D says that the second *B* in *BB* should be in lowercase. *BB* is an initialism that takes the first letter from each word in the name *Bakery Brothers*. Remember that all of the letters in initialisms must be capitalized, so *BB* is correctly capitalized. Choice D is incorrect.

EXAMPLE

Choose the correctly capitalized organization name.

a. National Association for People who Hate Taking Naps
b. Organization for The Most Interesting People in America
c. Club for High-School Students Who love Reading
d. Nebraskan Club for Mountain Climbers

Names of organizations follow the same capitalization rules as titles. Remember that when capitalizing titles, it is important to consider each word's part of speech. Nouns, pronouns, verbs, adjectives, and adverbs are always capitalized in titles. Consider the part of speech of every word in each answer choice.

In choice A, the capitalized words include adjectives, nouns, and verbs. These words are all correctly capitalized. *For* and *who* are in lowercase. Which parts of speech are these words? *For* is a preposition. Remember that short prepositions are not usually capitalized in titles, so leaving *for* in lowercase is acceptable. *Who* is a pronoun. Pronouns should always be capitalized in titles, so this is an error. Choice A is incorrect.

In choice B, there is an incorrectly capitalized word. An article should not be capitalized in a title unless it is the first word in the title. In this choice, *the* is capitalized in the middle of the title. This is an error, so choice B is incorrect.

In choice C, each capitalized word is correct. These words include nouns, adjectives, a pronoun, and a verb. *For* and *love* are in lowercase. Since *for* is a short preposition, it is acceptable to leave it in lowercase. However, *love* is a verb in this title. Verbs must be capitalized in titles, so this is an error. Choice C is incorrect.

In choice D, the capitalized words include adjectives and nouns. Words belonging to these parts of speech should always be capitalized in titles. The only word that is in lowercase is *for*, which may be left in lowercase because it is a short preposition. All of the words in this organization name are correctly capitalized or left in lowercase, so choice D is correct!

CHAPTER QUIZ

1. Every sentence always has a subject and a/an:

a. Imperative
b. Preposition
c. Predicate
d. Modifier

2. Which of the following sentences does NOT have an implied subject?

a. Take John on a quick walk.
b. Don't get lost.
c. John knows the way to the park.
d. Bring me back some flowers.

3. Which pronoun can be either singular or plural depending on what it is representing in the context of the sentence?

a. Nobody
b. Either
c. Several
d. All

4. Which of the following is written in third person perspective?

a. I am walking
b. He is walking
c. You are walking
d. We are walking

5. Which of the following best describes the function of an indirect object?

a. Shows how an action had an influence
b. Takes or receives the action of a verb
c. Explains or describes the subject
d. Shows that there is more information needed

6. Which of the following is a group of words that contains both a subject and a verb, and can be either independent or dependent?

a. Antecedent
b. Fragment
c. Phrase
d. Clause

7. Which of the following is an example of a complex sentence (as opposed to a simple or compound sentence)?

a. The time has come, and we are ready.
b. Judy and Alan watered the lawn and pulled weeds.
c. Marcia got married after she finished college.
d. I woke up at dawn; the sun was just coming up.

8. What method of correcting run-on sentences is the easiest way to make the sentence correct and more interesting at the same time?

a. Split into separate sentences
b. Join clauses properly
c. Reduce to one clause with a compound verb
d. Make one clause dependent

9. Which of the following is a word placed before a noun or pronoun that shows the relationship between an object and another word in the sentence?

a. Adjective
b. Adverb
c. Preposition
d. Conjunction

10. Which of the following should be put in single quotation marks?

a. Quote inside a quote
b. Indirect quote
c. Direct quote
d. All of the above

Chapter Quiz Answer Key

1. C: See section **Predicates**

2. C: See section **Subjects**

3. D: See section **Depend on Context**

4. B: See section **Person Agreement Examples**

5. A: See section **Indirect Objects**

6. D: See section **Clauses**

7. C: See section **Complex**

8. D: See section **Run-on Sentences**

9. C: See section **Prepositions**

10. A: See section **Quotation Marks**

Written Essay

Essays

Essays usually focus on one topic, subject, or goal. There are several types of essays, including informative, persuasive, and narrative. An essay's structure and formality depend on the type of essay and its goal. While narrative essays typically do not include outside sources, other types of essays often require some research and the use of primary and secondary sources.

The basic format of an essay typically has three major parts: the introduction, the body, and the conclusion. The body is further divided into the writer's main points. Most essays will have at least three main points, but essays that go into more depth can have almost any number of main points.

An essay's introduction should answer three questions:

1. What is the **subject** of the essay?

   If an essay is about a book, the answer would include the title and author of the book, as well as any additional information needed, such as the subject or argument of the book.

2. How does the essay **discuss** the subject?

   To answer this, the writer briefly summarizes the main points and the evidence supporting them to let readers know how the essay is organized and what information they can expect to read.

3. What will the essay **prove**?

This information is in the thesis statement, usually the opening paragraph's last sentence, which clearly states the writer's message.

The body elaborates on all the main points related to the thesis, introducing one main point at a time, and includes supporting evidence with each main point. Each body paragraph should state the point in a topic sentence, which is usually the first sentence in the paragraph. The paragraph should then explain the point's meaning, support it with quotations or other evidence, and then explain how this point and the evidence are related to the thesis. The writer should then repeat this procedure in a new paragraph for each additional main point.

The conclusion restates the content of the introduction, including the thesis, to remind the reader of the essay's main argument or subject. The essay writer may also summarize the highlights of the argument or description contained in the body of the essay, following the same organization originally used in the body. For example, a conclusion might look like: Point 1 + Point 2 + Point 3 = Thesis, or Point 1 → Point 2 → Point 3 → Thesis Proof. Good organization makes essays easier for writers to compose and provides a guide for readers to follow. Well-organized essays hold attention better and are more likely to get readers to believe or agree with the writer.

Using Sources in Essays

Sometimes writers use information from others in their work. This is most common in expository and persuasive writing. For an expository essay, a writer may not know all of the information that he or she needs to finish the composition. The writer may use other people's work to find the missing information and complete the composition. Persuasive writers may do research to find facts or statements from others that support their own beliefs and make their writing more persuasive. In both cases, research helps the writer find information that **supports** his or her **original work**.

Outside information must be relevant, true, and helpful to be appropriate for a composition. Writers must also be careful not to use too much outside information, since this can make the composition unoriginal. If a writer does use outside information, it is extremely important that the writer mention in the composition where the information came from. If the writer forgets or chooses not to say where the information came from, he or she has stolen someone else's work and presented it as their own. Doing this is called **plagiarism**.

Informational Texts

Informational texts, also called instructional or expository texts, are compositions written to inform the reader about a specific topic. An informational essay can inform readers in a variety of ways, such as giving them instructions, telling them facts about the topic, or teaching them why something happens. Informational texts should be logical, meaning that they should present information in an order that the reader can easily understand, and they should include the right amount of information so the writer successfully informs his or her audience of new information.

Informational texts should also focus on a **controlling idea**. In the introduction of an informational text, there may be a sentence or two that clearly state the essay's controlling idea. This sentence, or sentences, is called a **thesis statement**. The controlling idea should be clear throughout the composition. By emphasizing the controlling idea in the introduction, body, and conclusion, the writer can ensure that the controlling idea is clear. One way to make sure that the controlling idea is emphasized is to think about the purpose of each part of the essay. The introduction prepares the reader by telling them what the rest of the essay is about, so the controlling idea should be **introduced** in this section. The body tells the reader the information the writer wants to tell the audience, so this **explains** the controlling idea and facts about it to the reader. The conclusion is used to **remind** the reader of how the information in the body is related and **restates** the controlling idea one final time.

Review Video: Informational Text
Visit mometrix.com/academy and enter code: 924964

Structures or Organizational Patterns in Informational Texts

Informational text can be **descriptive**, meaning that it gives information that can be experienced through the five senses, or it answers the questions what, who, when, where, and why. One common method of organizing informational text is to put it in a certain sequence, or order. **Chronological** texts include events in the order that they occurred, from start to finish. **How-to**, or **instructional**, texts organize information into a series of instructions in the order in which the steps should be followed. **Comparison-contrast** structures of informational text describe different ideas to their readers by pointing out how things or ideas are similar and how they are different. **Cause and effect** structures of informational text describe events that occurred and the causes or reasons for those events. **Problem and solution** structures of informational texts introduce and describe problems and offer one or more solutions for each problem described.

Argumentative Writing

In argumentative writing, the writer expresses a belief or opinion that he or she wants to lead readers to agree with. When writing an argumentative composition, the writer should first identify the **topic** his or her opinion is about. The topic may be serious or fun, as long as there is one clear topic in the composition. The next step is for the writer to determine his or her opinion on the topic and determine why he or she holds that opinion. In order to persuade others to agree with their opinion, the writer must be able to give readers reasons to support the opinion. If the writer does not know why he or she has an opinion, it will be difficult to convince readers to agree. In addition to having reasons that support their opinion, writers should prepare examples that support each of these reasons in order to strengthen their composition.

Once the writer has determined his or her topic, opinion, and reasons for having the opinion, he or she is ready to begin writing an argumentative essay. In the introduction, the writer should capture the reader's interest, introduce the topic, and reveal his or her opinion about the topic. In the body of the composition, the writer should remind the reader of the opinion and give his or her reasons for holding the opinion. If the writer has any examples, facts, or other information that supports his or her opinion or reasons for believing it, these should also be included in the body. Writers may also use a body paragraph to mention opposing opinions or beliefs and explain why they disagree with them. As in other compositions, the conclusion should remind the reader of the essay's topic and purpose, as well as remind the reader how the opinion has been explained and supported. The conclusion should also invite the reader to continue thinking about the topic and writer's opinion. This can be done through questions or statements that lead readers to consider whether or not they agree with the author's opinion or what their own opinions are.

Review Video: Argumentative Writing
Visit mometrix.com/academy and enter code: 561544

Informative vs. Persuasive Writing

Informative writing, also called explanatory or expository writing, is written to show that something is true or factual, while **persuasive** writing is written to lead the reader to agree with something that may or may not be true or factual. While persuasive text is written to **persuade** readers to agree with the author's position, informative text simply **provides information** to readers. Informative writing **informs** readers about why or how something is as it is. This can include offering new information, explaining how a process works, or describing a concept for readers.

Facts and Opinions

Writers and readers must always be aware of the difference between fact and opinion. A **fact** can be tested and proven to be true. An **opinion**, on the other hand, is someone's personal thoughts or feelings. Opinions are often not changed by information. If an author writes that a newborn elephant is about five times taller than a newborn giraffe, then he or she is stating a fact. If the author writes that giraffes are more interesting than elephants, then he or she is giving an opinion because this cannot be proven to be true or false. Opinions are often supported by facts. For instance, the author might use a comparison between the way that giraffes eat and the way elephants eat as evidence of how giraffes are more interesting. An opinion supported by facts tends to be more convincing. On the other hand, when authors support their opinions with other opinions, readers should seriously think about and read the argument carefully to see whether it is logical and trustworthy.

Review Video: Distinguishing Fact and Opinion
Visit mometrix.com/academy and enter code: 870899

Responding to a Text

An essay prompt may require writers to write about a text they have read. When writing an essay like this, writers should show that they understand the text they have read. They may mention their own thoughts, ideas, and opinions in the essay. However, the main idea of the essay should be about the text mentioned in the prompt.

When planning the essay, writers should consider what the text is about and how it is written. Writers should identify the purpose, main idea, and structure of the text. For informational and persuasive texts, they should also think about the supporting details the author used in the text. All of these facts about the text will help writers understand the text well and allow the writer to create a response to the text.

Responding to Multiple Texts

Essay prompts may ask writers to write about more than one text. In this case, writers should identify the purpose, main idea, and structure of each text. They should also look at the kinds of supporting details that the author of each text uses. Once writers know these details, they should think about the differences and similarities between the texts. The main ideas of each text may oppose each other, or one may support the other. Writers will need to write about both texts in the essay, so they must understand both texts and the connection between the texts.

Chapter Quiz

1. What type of essay does NOT typically include outside sources?

a. Expository
b. Informative
c. Persuasive
d. Narrative

2. Which of the following is NOT true of informational texts?

a. Informational texts are also called instructional or expository texts
b. Informational texts should be logical
c. Informational texts should focus on a central idea
d. Informational texts can only be structured chronologically

3. In an argumentative essay, which of the following should be included in the body?

a. A reminder of the writer's opinion and his or her reasons for holding the opinion
b. Examples, facts, or other information that supports the writer's opinion
c. Opposing opinions or beliefs and explanations of why the writer disagrees with them
d. All of the above

Chapter Quiz Answer Key

1. D: See section **Essays**

2. D: See section **Structures or Organizational Patterns in Informational Texts**

3. D: See section **Argumentative Writing**

Informational Text Example

Below is a prompt for an informational text. There is also an example of an essay that addresses the prompt. There are multiple drafts of this essay to show what kinds of changes a writer may make during the writing process to improve his or her work.

Prompt:

One of the things that makes each person unique is the hobbies they enjoy doing in their free time. Write about a hobby you enjoy. Be sure to include information about how you became interested in the hobby.

ROUGH DRAFT

Prepare to see your boredom disappear before your very eyes! Presto! That is what my favorite hobby did for me. Learning and performing magic tricks for my friends and family is my favorite hobby.

Every time we go to my grandparents' house, he does a card trick when we get there. Last year on my birthday, he gave me a cool deck of cards and showed me how to do a trick. I practiced it a couple of times and then tried it with some of my friends. I did it correctly with most of them, and they were so impressed! I was looking up new card tricks online when I discovered that there are other kinds of magic tricks, too. I decided to learn one to show my grandpa the next time he visited. I ended up learning five tricks that day! Since then, learning magic tricks has been my hobby.

Before I started learning magic tricks, my hobby was collecting rocks. I started collecting rocks around my neighborhood, but then I also started collecting them on vacations. I enjoyed that hobby until school started again. Then I had fewer opportunities to find cool rocks. I enjoy learning magic tricks much more, and it is something I can do any day after school. I also like learning magic tricks more that collecting things because it is more exciting. Looking at the rocks I had collected got old, but I never get tired of magic tricks!

One of my favorite things about my hobby is that I can perform magic shows. Once I have learned several new magic tricks, I get to do a magic show for my parents and my sister. If there was ever a talent show at school, I would do magic tricks as my talent. It is fun to show off the tricks I have learned, but my favorite part of doing magic shows is seeing that others enjoy my magic tricks. I love that I can share my hobby with others!

I am very thankful to my grandpa for inspiring my hobby! I believe I will always love doing magic tricks and hope I can become a better magician if I keep learning and practicing!

Revised Draft

Prepare to see your boredom disappear before your very eyes! Presto! That is what my favorite hobby did for me. Learning and performing magic tricks for my friends and family is my favorite hobby.

Every time we go to my grandparents' house, he does a card trick when we get there. Last year on my birthday, he gave me a cool deck of cards and showed me how to do a trick. I practiced it a couple of times and then tried it with some of my friends. I did it correctly with most of them, and they were so impressed! I was looking up new card tricks online when I discovered that there are other kinds of magic tricks, too. I decided to learn one to show my grandpa the next time he visited. I ended up learning five tricks that day! Since then, learning magic tricks has been my hobby.

~~Before I started learning magic tricks, my hobby was collecting rocks. I started collecting rocks around my neighborhood, but then I also started collecting them on vacations. I enjoyed that hobby until school started again. Then I had fewer opportunities to find cool rocks. I enjoy learning magic tricks much more, and it is something I can do any day after school. I also like learning magic tricks more that collecting things because it is more exciting. Looking at the rocks I had collected got old, but I never get tired of magic tricks!~~

One of my favorite things about my hobby is that I can perform magic shows. Once I have learned several new magic tricks, I get to do a magic show for my parents and my sister. If there was ever a talent show at school, I would do magic tricks as my talent. It is fun to show off the tricks I have learned, but my favorite part of doing magic shows is seeing that others enjoy my magic tricks. I love that I can share my hobby with others!

I still enjoy watching others do magic tricks, but I enjoy learning and performing them even more. I am very thankful to my grandpa for inspiring my hobby! I believe I will always love doing magic tricks and hope I can become a better magician if I keep learning and practicing!

Revised Draft Notes

Remember the purpose of the revising stage of the writing process. When revising, it is important to look at the whole composition. Do all of the paragraphs strengthen the composition? Do the introduction and conclusion help the reader understand the controlling idea and main points?

First, look at the underlined words. These are words that have been added. In the conclusion, a sentence has been added. This sentence strengthens the composition because it creates a transition from the body to the conclusion. It also gives the writer's thoughts about the details he or she included in the essay. Before, the conclusion began abruptly and only mentioned one of the writer's points from the body of the composition. After this sentence was added, the conclusion became about each of the writer's points from the body paragraphs. This sentence reminds the reader of the writer's points and the composition's controlling idea, instead of focusing on only one of the writer's points.

Next, look at what has been crossed out in this essay. These are words that have been removed. A whole paragraph has been omitted! Why is that? There were no huge errors, and the writing made sense. The paragraph talks about why learning magic tricks is better than the writer's former hobby. While this is related to the controlling idea, this information is not entirely relevant and does not offer much new information about magic tricks. This paragraph does not strengthen the composition or help the reader understand the controlling idea. The writer made a wise choice to remove this information and should later replace it with a paragraph that gives the reader new information about the writer's hobby, why the writer enjoys it, or something the writer has experienced through it.

Edited Draft

Prepare to see your boredom disappear before your very eyes! Presto! ~~That is what my favorite hobby did for me.~~ Learning and performing magic tricks for my friends and family is my favorite hobby.

My interest in magic tricks was inspired by my grandpa. Every time we go to my grandparents' house, he does a card trick when we get there. Last year on my birthday, he gave me a cool deck of cards and showed me how to do a trick. I practiced it a couple of times and then tried it with some of my friends. I did it correctly with most of them, and they were so impressed! I was looking up new card tricks online when I discovered that there are other kinds of magic tricks, too. I decided to learn one to show my grandpa the next time he visited. I ended up learning five tricks that day! Since then, learning magic tricks has been my hobby.

~~Before I started learning magic tricks, my hobby was collecting rocks. I started collecting rocks around my neighborhood, but then I also started collecting them on vacations. I enjoyed that hobby until school started again. Then I had fewer opportunities to find cool rocks. I enjoy learning magic tricks much more, and it is something I can do any day after school. I also like learning magic tricks more that collecting things because it is more exciting. Looking at the rocks I had collected got old, but I never get tired of magic tricks!~~

One of my favorite things about my hobby is that I can perform magic shows. Once I have learned several new magic tricks, I get to do a magic show for my parents and my sister. ~~If there was ever a talent show at school, I would do magic tricks as my talent.~~ My sister wants me to do a magic show at her birthday party. I am so excited to do my magic tricks for a new audience! It is fun to show off the tricks I have learned, but my favorite part of doing magic shows is seeing that others enjoy my magic tricks. I love that I can share my hobby with others!

I still enjoy watching others do magic tricks, but I enjoy learning and performing them even more. I am very thankful to my grandpa for inspiring my hobby! I believe I will always love doing magic tricks and hope I can become a better magician if I keep learning and practicing!

EDITED DRAFT NOTES

Since the writer has revised his or her work, the next step is to edit the composition. Remember that editing is very similar to revising, but editing usually includes paying attention to each paragraph, instead of the whole composition. Look at the changes that were made to each paragraph.

In the introduction, a sentence was removed. Why was it removed? While it said something about hobbies, it did not strengthen the composition. This sentence connects the hook to the prompt, but it does not introduce the topic or give the reader useful information. This sentence is not about the specific hobby being discussed in the composition. While it gives a transition from the hook to the thesis, a different sentence would better prepare the reader for the information in the rest of the essay.

Only one change has been made in the second paragraph. A transition has been added to the beginning of the first sentence. This helps connect this paragraph to the rest of the composition and prepares the reader for the information in the paragraph. Before, this paragraph simply described an event and explained how it led the writer to begin his or her hobby. However, the reader is not told why the paragraph is relevant until later in the paragraph. Now, the reader is told the purpose at the beginning of the paragraph. This strengthens the composition by improving how this paragraph flows with the rest of the essay.

What has been changed in the fourth paragraph? Another sentence has been crossed out, and two new ones have been added. Why? This paragraph tells why the writer enjoys doing magic shows, and it includes the example of magic shows the writer has performed for his or her family. The end of the paragraph tells the reasons why the writer has enjoyed doing the magic shows. The crossed-out sentence tells the reader that the author would do a magic act for a school talent show. This detail is relevant to the rest of the paragraph, but it does not support the paragraph's main point. The underlined sentences include supporting details that explain that the writer has an opportunity to do a show for a new audience. This example is better because it elaborates on the first example and connects the examples to the reason the writer enjoys doing magic shows. These sentences help the paragraph flow better and support the other ideas in the paragraph.

The remaining marks are left to remind the writer that the third paragraph still needs to be replaced. This information will be added before the final draft is finished.

FINAL DRAFT

Prepare to see your boredom disappear before your very eyes! Presto! That is what happened to me when I began learning how to do magic tricks. Now, learning and performing magic tricks for my friends and family is my favorite hobby.

My interest in magic tricks was inspired by my grandpa. Every time we go to my grandparents' house, he does a card trick when we get there. Last year on my birthday, he gave me a cool deck of cards and showed me how to do a trick. I practiced it a couple of times and then tried it with some of my friends. I did it correctly with most of them, and they were so impressed! I was looking up new card tricks online when I discovered that there are other kinds of magic tricks, too. I decided to learn one to show my grandpa the next time he visited. I ended up learning five tricks that day! Since then, magic tricks have been my hobby.

While doing magic tricks is very fun, it takes practice at first. Some tricks are difficult to get the hang of because you have to do some steps very carefully. For example, for some tricks, you have to hide a small object in your hand or behind your hand. If the object is not completely hidden or if you make it too obvious that you are hiding something, the trick does not work as well. These tricks are very difficult for me to learn, so I have to practice them more than other tricks. Sometimes it takes patience, but mastering a trick is so fun that practicing is worth it!

One of my favorite things about my hobby is that I can perform magic shows. Once I have learned several new magic tricks, I get to do a magic show for my parents and my sister. My sister wants me to do a magic show at her birthday party. I am so excited to do my magic tricks for a new audience! It is fun to show off the tricks I have learned, but my favorite part of doing magic shows is seeing that others enjoy my magic tricks. I love that I can share my hobby with others!

I still enjoy watching others do magic tricks, but I enjoy learning and performing them even more. I am very thankful to my grandpa for inspiring my hobby! I believe I will always love doing magic tricks and hope I can become a better magician if I keep learning and practicing!

FINAL DRAFT NOTES

This is the final draft! In this draft, information has been added to the introduction, and there is a new paragraph. Now, the introduction includes a sentence that introduces the controlling idea of the composition and prepares the reader for the information in the rest of the essay. The new paragraph also gives new information about doing magic tricks. This paragraph describes a lesson the writer learned through doing magic tricks and gives the reader more information about the writer's experience practicing the hobby. These additions strengthen the composition by replacing weaker information with details that are more informative and engaging for the reader.

EVALUATION

The essay answers the prompt and is on topic throughout the composition. The controlling idea is clear and is stated in the introduction, supported in the body, and restated in the conclusion. The thesis statement restates parts of the prompt and gives the reader a preview of the rest of the essay. The body uses well-structured paragraphs to explain the supporting details and examples and connects them to the controlling idea. The conclusion also emphasizes the controlling idea and supporting details and invites the reader to consider what they have read.

The essay is also interesting and written with a variety of sentence types. It uses transitions and good paragraph structure to make the essay easy for the reader to understand. The introduction also uses a hook to get the reader's attention and help him or her relate to the information in the essay. Not only does this essay answer the prompt and have appropriate structure, but it also makes use of good, engaging, and interesting details.

Practice Test #1

Reading

Sticky Water

(1) News flash: water is sticky. This is a surprise to many people because water does not seem sticky. In fact, it's the first thing that people reach for to wash away stickiness and any other kind of dirt. The second item, of course, is soap.

(2) Water and things like glue are sticky in different ways. Glue is sticky in two ways. Water is sticky in only one way. Glue feels and acts sticky. It is used to join objects such as paper, wood, and plastic together. Water does not feel or act sticky.

(3) Glue is sticky in two ways. One way is called adhesion. This is when glue, after it is poured on a surface, spreads into tiny holes and dents and hardens. The glue holds the surfaces together like the pieces of a jigsaw puzzle. However, for glue to work well, it also needs to stick to itself and hold together. This is called cohesion.

(4) Water does not have adhesion. If you pour it on a piece of wood, the wood will absorb the water, but water will not harden to make two things stick together. Water does have cohesion. Water is a unique substance made up of two elements: hydrogen (H) and oxygen (O). Water is made up of two parts hydrogen and one part oxygen. The formula for water is H2O. The hydrogen atoms not only stick to the oxygen, but also to other water molecules, much in the same way magnets stick to metal. Water molecules stick to each other because of "hydrogen bonds." If water did not hold together, it could not be a liquid. It would boil and turn into steam.

(5) To see the "stickiness" of water, try the following experiment. This experiment is not dangerous, and it only requires ordinary objects that you probably have at home. However, you will end up spilling some water, so ask an adult if it is okay to do the experiment before starting.

Sticky Water EXPERIMENT

You will need the following for this experiment:

- One short plastic cup
- One small pitcher of water
- At least 20 pennies
- A sponge or rag for spills

1. First, fill the plastic cup with water from the pitcher. Make sure to fill the cup all the way up to the rim. Don't spill any water! If you spill water, wipe it up. Make sure the very full glass is sitting on a dry spot.
2. Next, carefully slip a penny into the cup and look closely. Did any of the water spill over the edge? Probably not. Continue adding pennies slowly to avoid splashing. Slip them in gently. Do not throw them in.
3. Keep putting in pennies until water spills over the edge.

How many pennies did it take for the water to spill over? It was probably more than you thought. Most people who do this experiment think one or two pennies will make the very full glass spill, but usually it takes more than 10 pennies. The explanation for this is cohesion. Each time you put in a penny, the water molecules hold on tighter and tighter to each other. Finally, when there is absolutely no more room in the glass and they're hanging over the edge of the glass, the water spills. One time, a scientist was able to get 25 pennies into the glass before it spilled! Now that's sticky water!

Refer to the passage "Sticky Water" to answer questions 1-9.

1. What does the word *absorb* mean, as used in paragraph 4?

a. To soak up
b. To become darker
c. To push away
d. To make sticky

2. Which sentence from the passage best demonstrates that water performs differently than glue?

a. If you pour it on a piece of wood, the wood will absorb the water, but the water will not harden to make things stick together.
b. Finally, when there is absolutely no more room in the glass and they're hanging over the edge of the glass, the water spills.
c. The hydrogen atoms not only stick to the oxygen, but also to other water molecules, much in the same way magnets stick to metal.
d. Water is a unique substance made up of two elements: hydrogen (H) and oxygen (O).

3. Which key idea is supported by the information in paragraph 3?

a. Glue is neither a solid nor a liquid.
b. Water has unique chemical properties.
c. Water is used to clean surfaces.
d. There are multiple ways for a substance to be sticky.

4. What conclusion can the reader make about the Sticky Water Experiment?

a. Other liquids besides water would behave in the same way if they were used in the experiment.
b. The same number of pennies will make the water spill each time.
c. Throwing the pennies in might make the water spill sooner.
d. Glue is made of the same elements as water.

5. What is the central idea of "Sticky Water"?

a. Not all science experiments are dangerous.
b. Glue is sticky in multiple ways.
c. Water is used to wash away stickiness.
d. Water is sticky in a way people do not expect.

6. How do paragraphs 3 and 4 help the reader understand the stickiness of water?

a. By explaining multiple uses for water
b. By describing what to do with water in the experiment
c. By comparing the qualities of glue to the qualities of water
d. By arguing that water is the best things to use when washing sticky things

7. What is most likely the author's purpose for writing "Sticky Water"?

a. To provide a sequence of events that resulted in a discovery about water
b. To argue that water is the most unique substance
c. To explain the sticky qualities of water due to cohesion
d. To suggest that the reader try other experiments involving water

8. What can the reader infer based on the section "Sticky Water Experiment"?

a. Adding pennies to a cup of glue will cause the glue to spill.
b. The experiment could also be done with other small objects.
c. The stickiness of water can be shown through many experiments.
d. Adhesion and cohesion are different names for the same thing.

9. How does the bulleted list under "Sticky Water Experiment" help the reader understand the experiment?

a. It provides the reader with step-by-step instructions.
b. It gives the reader the list of items needed for the experiment.
c. It uses similes that help the reader imagine what water molecules look like.
d. It shows the reader that the experiment is easy and safe to complete at home.

My Shadow

by Robert Louis Stevenson

I have a little shadow that goes in and out with me,
And what can be the use of him is more than I can see.
He is very, very like me from the heels up to the head;
And I see him jump before me, when I jump into my bed.
The funniest thing about him is the way he likes to grow—
Not at all like proper children, which is always very slow;
For he sometimes shoots up taller like an India-rubber ball,
And he sometimes gets so little that there's none of him at all.
He hasn't got a notion of how children ought to play,
And can only make a fool of me in every sort of way.
He stays so close beside me, he's a coward, you can see;
I'd think shame to stick to nursie as that shadow sticks to me!
One morning, very early, before the sun was up,
I rose and found the shining dew on every buttercup;
But my lazy little shadow, like an errant sleepy-head,
Had stayed at home behind me and was fast asleep in bed.

Refer to the passage "My Shadow" to answer questions 10-15.

10. Lines 5 through 8 support the key idea that:

a. The shadow is purposely teasing the speaker.
b. The speaker's shadow can only be seen during the day.
c. The speaker thinks that his shadow is being silly.
d. The speaker's shadow is not always the same size as the speaker.

11. The author's use of personification in lines 9 through 12 of "My Shadow" helps demonstrate that:

a. The shadow does not like the speaker.
b. The shadow is able to speak.
c. The shadow seems to have a mind of its own.
d. The shadow is a trickster.

12. Based on the speaker's descriptions in the poem, which two statements describe how the speaker thinks of his shadow? Select all that may apply.

a. The speaker hopes that he and his shadow can be friends.
b. The speaker does not understand the behavior of his shadow.
c. The speaker worries that his shadow is lonely.
d. The speaker is afraid of his shadow.
e. The speaker believes the shadow has negative qualities.

13. Which sentence from the poem shows that the shadow moves with the speaker?

a. He hasn't got a notion of how children ought to play
b. Had stayed at home behind me and was fast asleep in bed
c. For he sometimes shoots up taller like an India-rubber ball
d. And I see him jump before me, when I jump into my bed

14. The author says his shadow is "like an India-rubber ball," which is similar to a bouncy ball. With that knowledge, what is most likely the reason the author used the simile "like an India-rubber ball" to describe his shadow?

a. To show how suddenly the shadow's height can increase
b. To show that the shadow is round, like a ball
c. To show that the speaker wants the shadow to play with him
d. To show that the shadow can be tinier than a toy ball

15. Based on lines 13 through 16, what can the reader conclude about the speaker's shadow?

a. The speaker's shadow can be seen at any time of day.
b. The speaker's shadow stayed home because he was upset.
c. The speaker's shadow cannot be seen when there is no light.
d. The speaker's shadow has become boring to him.

A Garden in the Desert

(1) Barry lives one street up and four houses down from his best friend, Manolo. Barry, his parents, and his older brother Ricardo have lived in the small ranch house for as long as he can remember. Manolo's family moved into their house a few months before Manolo was born. At that time, 10 years ago, their housing development was only five square blocks. About 250 small, one-story houses dotted the streets. Today, their housing development is three times as big and is considered an actual neighborhood. It is called Cypress Heights.

(2) There are no cypresses or any other kinds of trees in Cypress Heights. The neighborhood was built near a desert. It has no heights and no hills – just flat stretches of paved road and concrete sidewalks. Grass sprouts up between the cracks in the sidewalks but refuses to take root on lawns. Flowers also have a hard time growing in Barry and Manolo's hot and dusty neighborhood. The only plants that grow around most of the houses are patches of ragged-looking weeds.

(3) In contrast to the dusty lawns, most of the ranch houses are very well kept. The outsides of the houses are freshly painted, and many lawns are decorated with bird baths and patio furniture. The lack of gardens and lawns, however, makes the neighborhood look dusty, downtrodden, and old. Without grass roots to knit a protective net in the soil, the wind picks up dirt and blows it all over the roads, roofs, and sidewalks. After a windy day, everything in Cypress Heights is covered in brown and gray dust.

(4) Manolo and Barry love living in Cypress Heights because their houses are so close, and each boy can easily get to the other's house. A short fence surrounds Manolo's backyard. Manolo can jump over the fence and walk along the path in the neighbor's backyard to Barry's street. From there, Manolo can walk past three houses to get to Barry's. The fence around Barry's backyard is too high to jump over and too smooth to climb, so Barry has to stick to the streets to get to Manolo's house.

(5) One summer day, Barry rode his bike over to Manolo's house. He brought a backpack with a picnic lunch. "Let's go to the playground at the school," said Barry. "I have two peanut butter and jelly sandwiches and two juice boxes for lunch. We can stay there all afternoon."

(6) "Sounds good," said Manolo. His older sister was watching him while his mother was at work. He asked his sister, Rosa, for permission.

(7) "Just be back before five o'clock," said Rosa. "Mom should be home by then."

(8) Barry and Manolo's school was about a mile away. It was a long, brown, one-story building with big windows and a large play set in the front. In the back were two sets of train tracks. Usually, the trains only ran at night, but every so often a freight train would pass the school during the day, making the windows rattle and the children rush from their seats to watch it.

(9) On their way to the schoolyard, they passed a house that had just been sold a few weeks earlier. In the yard, instead of dusty weeds, was white gravel. Dotted around the lawn were different cactus plants. Barry and Manolo stopped their bikes and stared at the lawn in surprise. "Wow, this yard looks great," said Barry. "But I don't

want cactus plants in my yard. What if you ran into one while playing tag? That would hurt!"

(10) "There are other plants that work in this area," said a voice from behind a large cactus.

(11) A woman with short brown hair stepped out from behind the cactus and walked over to Barry and Manolo. She had a wide-brimmed hat on her head. "We planted cacti because they don't need much water," said the woman with a smile. She waved her hand toward her house. "It is too expensive to water plants or a lawn. But there are other drought-resistant plants that will do well here."

(12) "What kind of plant is 'drought resistant'?" asked Manolo.

(13) "Basically, it is a plant that doesn't need much water," said the woman. "Plants like lavender, aloe, lamb's ear, and oriental yew are also drought-resistant. I have some of those in pots ready to be planted. If you promise to take care of them, I can give you some to plant in your yards."

(14) "Sure!" said Barry and Manolo at once.

(15) The woman motioned to the boys to follow her behind her house. She put several small plants in a low, flat box attached to the back of her bicycle. She strapped down the plants and climbed on the seat. "Lead the way," she said.

(16) "Thank you," said Barry. "By the way, I'm Barry and this is Manolo."

(17) "I'm Mrs. Juarez," said the woman. "Nice to meet you."

(18) "Wait a minute," said Barry. "You just moved in. Shouldn't we give presents to you?"

(19) "That's okay," laughed Mrs. Juarez. "I don't have any more room in my garden, so you are doing me a favor by taking them. But I will accept a cold drink after the bike ride!"

(20) "Sounds good," said Barry. The three of them headed towards the boys' houses, ready to break ground on their new gardens.

An Artist Thinking BIG

(1) A sculpture can be made in many different sizes, from very tiny to very large. The largest sculptures are carved from whole mountains! Three such mountain carvings have been done in the United States. Two are complete, and one is still being carved today.

(2) One artist, Gutzon Borglum, has a connection to all three sculptures.

(3) Borglum first worked on Stone Mountain in Georgia. The Daughters of the Confederacy, a group of women whose ancestors were Rebel soldiers in the Civil War, asked Borglum to carve a 20-foot-high bust of southern General Robert E. Lee in 1915. Borglum talked them into a much bigger bas-relief, or shallow relief, project, but before it could be finished, he fought with the Daughters and left. It was finished by Augustus Lukeman and Walter Hancock and completed in 1972. Although Gutzon Borglum did not finish this mountain, he developed techniques such as a giant magic lantern projector to cast a drawing onto a mountain. Later he would use this technique on another famous carved mountain.

(4) The most famous mountain carving is Mount Rushmore in South Dakota. The mountain has the faces of four famous and beloved American Presidents. George Washington, Thomas Jefferson, Theodore Roosevelt, and Abraham Lincoln look down from an enormous mountain in the Black Hills. Gutzon Borglum started the project in 1927 and continued working on carving the four 60-foot-high statues until his death in 1941. His son, Lincoln Borglum, finished the mountain carving.

(5) The third mountain carving is also in South Dakota, a short drive away from Mount Rushmore. The Crazy Horse Memorial, when finished, will be the largest sculpture in the world at 563 feet tall and 641 feet long. In 1939, Gutzon Borglum had an assistant artist named Korczack Ziolkowski working with him on the Mount Rushmore project. Chief Henry Standing Bear of the Lakota Sioux tribe asked Ziolkowski to carve the monument to show that Native Americans had heroes, too. Ziolkowski worked on the sculpture until his death in 1982. Now his wife Ruth and seven of their ten children are working to finish it.

(6) Gutzon Borglum, and the artists that followed him, show us that no dreams are too big to become reality. One man, with the right vision, can change the world.

Refer to the passage "A Garden in the Desert" to answer questions 16-19.

16. In paragraph 3, the word *downtrodden* is used to describe Barry and Manolo's neighborhood. Based on the word's suffix and the way it is used in the story, what does *downtrodden* mean in paragraph 3?

a. An upsetting place to live
b. Having a distressed appearance
c. Having many walking paths
d. Located low in a valley

17. What is the effect of the author using a third-person omniscient point of view for this story?

a. The reader understands that Mrs. Juarez is the owner of the garden.
b. The reader knows what Cypress Heights looks like.
c. The reader understands why Mrs. Juarez planted drought-resistant plants.
d. The reader knows how Barry and Manolo feel about living in Cypress Heights.

18. In paragraph 11, Mrs. Juarez explains that drought-resistant plants can do well in the neighborhood. How does this support the theme of the passage?

a. It shows Barry and Manolo that the unexpected is possible.
b. It shows Barry and Manolo the value of generosity.
c. It shows Barry and Manolo that they can have a lifelong friendship.
d. It shows Barry and Manolo how to overcome a challenge.

19. Which sentence is the best description of Barry and Manolo's relationship with Mrs. Juarez by the end of the story?

a. Barry and Manolo are worried about Mrs. Juarez because she is near cactus plants.
b. Barry and Manolo are frustrated with Mrs. Juarez for interrupting their bike ride.
c. Barry and Manolo are grateful to Mrs. Juarez for giving them new plants.
d. Barry and Manolo are eager to show Mrs. Juarez their school playground.

Refer to the passage "An Artist Thinking BIG" to answer questions 20-21.

20. How does the author use the structure of "An Artist Thinking BIG" to achieve his or her purpose?

a. By explaining the causes and effect of the delays on the Crazy Horse Memorial
b. By describing the experience of creating large mountain carvings
c. By persuading the reader to try creating a sculpture of their own
d. By describing the history behind three mountain carvings found in America

21. Why did the author include the picture of Mount Rushmore in the passage?

a. To show the appearance of Gutzon Borglum's carving at Mount Rushmore
b. To compare the size of Mount Rushmore to Gutzon Borglum's other mountain carvings
c. To emphasize the carving techniques that were used in Mount Rushmore
d. To provide a step-by-step process on how Mount Rushmore was carved

Refer to the passages "A Garden in the Desert" and "An Artist Thinking BIG" to answer questions 22-24.

22. This question has two parts. After you answer Part A, answer Part B:

Part A: How is Mrs. Juarez in "A Garden in the Desert" similar to Gutzon Borglum in "An Artist Thinking BIG"?

a. She uses sculpture to make something beautiful.
b. She wants many people to come and see her creation.
c. She thinks creatively to produce something eye-catching.
d. She works for many years to complete her project.

Part B: Which of the following sentences from "A Garden in the Desert" supports the answer to Part A?

a. "Basically, it is a plant that doesn't need much water," said the woman.
b. "We planted cacti because they don't need much water," said the woman with a smile.
c. Dotted around the lawn were different cactus plants.
d. On their way to the schoolyard, they passed a house that had just been sold a few weeks earlier.

23. What is different about Mrs. Juarez's garden in "A Garden in the Desert" and Gutzon Borglum's sculptures in "An Artist Thinking BIG"?

a. Mrs. Juarez's garden could only be planted in a place that had a lot of water, but Gutzon Borglum's sculptures could be made anywhere.
b. The cost of Mrs. Juarez's garden did not concern her, but the cost of Gutzon Borglum's mountain sculptures concerned him.
c. Mrs. Juarez's garden inspired Barry and Manolo to plant their own gardens, but Gutzon Borglum's mountain sculptures did not lead to any other sculptures.
d. Mrs. Juarez planted her garden using plants and common tools, but Gutzon Borglum needed special tools and skills to create his mountain sculptures.

24. Which idea is supported in both "A Garden in the Desert" and "An Artist Thinking BIG"?

a. Friendship can form from everyday events.
b. Opportunities to create beauty are all around.
c. Mentors often help their students do great things.
d. No landscape is without beauty if you know where to look.

Extended Response

Your STAAR test will include the following instructions for your extended response question. The response prompts used here are similar to the prompts you will see on the STAAR test.

25. Read the passage "A Garden in the Desert." Based on the passage, write a response to the following:

Explain how Mrs. Juarez is a generous character.

Write a well-organized informational composition that uses specific evidence from the passage to support your answer.

Remember to —

- clearly state your central idea
- organize your writing
- develop your ideas in detail
- use evidence from the selection in your response
- use correct spelling, capitalization, punctuation, and grammar

Manage your time carefully so that you can —

- review the selection
- plan your response
- write your response
- revise and edit your response

Revising

Shiloh wrote this narrative paper about a boy named Simon and his father. Read the following paper and note the revisions that Shiloh should make. Once you have read her paper, answer the questions that follow it.

Simon and His Father

(1) "Well, that about does it," said Simon, gluing the last decal on the rudder of his model B17G Flying Fortress plane.

(2) "We have to let the glue dry," said Pedro, looking down at the finished plane.

(3) "While we're waiting, let's go get your car," said Simon. (4) "It's only three o'clock, so the store is still open."

(5) "I'll go home and get my money," said Pedro, and then he left.

(6) Pedro was getting his money, Simon looked at his newly finished plane. (7) He and Pedro had spent about four hours building it. (8) It was the first time Simon had ever built a model airplane without his father's help. (9) His father had offered, but this time Simon said he wanted to try it on his own. (10) Pedro read the directions and handed Simon parts while Simon looked over Pedro's shoulder at the plans and carefully glued the pieces in place. (11) It was the hardest model Simon had ever built.

(12) Just then there was a knock on the door.

(13) "Can I come in?" asked Simon's father.

(14) "Sure," said Simon. (15) "Check out the plane!"

(16) "Wow," said Simon's father quietly, looking closely at the finished model. (17) "You and Pedro did a great job. (18) It looks just like the real thing."

(19) At that moment it occurred to Simon that his father, behind the proud smile, might feel hurt because Simon let Pedro help him after telling his father he wanted to build it alone. (20) "You're not mad?" Simon asked.

(21) "Mad?" asked Simon's father. (22) "About what?"

(23) "That I asked Pedro to help me after you offered," said Simon, taking his eyes from his father's face and looking at the model.

(24) "Simon," said his father, "of course I'm not mad. (25) I'm proud. (26) You and Pedro did a great job! (27) I think I can take some credit for teaching you, but this shows that you are ready to start tackling these kinds of projects on your own. (28) Or, of course, with a friend."

(29) "Thanks, Dad," said Simon, giving his father a hug. (30) "You did teach me a lot of things. (31) A few of them I remembered when the plane we were building. (32) Pedro knows a lot, too."

(33) "Speaking of Pedro, there's the doorbell," said Simon's father, giving Simon a quick last squeeze. (34) "Would you two like a ride to the store this time? (35) It is pretty heavy this time of day."

(36) "Yes, the traffic probably would be a lot worse now, so we could use a ride," said Simon. (37) "Thanks, Dad."

(38) "No problem," said Simon's father. (39) "I'll get the keys."

26. Which word would be the best to add to the beginning of sentence 6 to improve the transition?

a. Until
b. While
c. Because
d. Whether

27. Which of the following would be an effective supporting detail to add after sentence 9?

a. Simon did not think his dad could help him, so he asked Pedro to help because he had built more models.
b. Simon had been hoping to build the plane on his own, but Pedro was upset when he learned this.
c. But, when Pedro offered to stay and work with him, Simon decided that he could use Pedro's help.
d. However, Pedro said that Simon would need help, so Simon listened to Pedro and let him help instead.

28. Which of the following is the best revision of sentence 31?

a. A few of them, when we were building the plane, I remembered.
b. When the plane we were building I remembered a few of them.
c. I remembered a few of them when we were building the plane.
d. We were building the plane when I remembered a few of them.

29. Sentence 35 uses unclear wording. Choose the word that should be used instead of *it*.

________ is pretty heavy this time of day.

Planes
Models
Money
Traffic

Brandon wrote this informational paper about an uncommon method of gardening. Read the following paper and note the revisions that Brandon should make. Once you have read his paper, answer the questions that follow it.

Creative Gardening

(1) With more and more cities appearing in America, having a backyard garden is getting more and more difficult. (2) Instead, those who want a garden are creating balcony gardens by squeezing a few plants, or even a dwarf fruit tree, into what small space they have available. (3) While many plants are adaptable to different locations, plants should be chosen based on the area the garden will be in.

(4) Sunlight is very important. (5) Plants need the Sun to perform photosynthesis. (6) However, some plants need more than others. (7) This means that a shady porch and a sunny balcony will be better for different plants. (8) An area that receives less than six hours of sunlight each day is considered "partial shade." (9) Vegetables, such as beets, carrots, and peas, and decorative plants, such as hostas, begonias, and violas, may thrive here. (10) Some plants do not do well at all in patio and balcony gardens. (11) Full-shade areas receive less than three hours of daily sunlight. (12) Some ferns and types of ivy suffer without much Sun. (13) However, gardeners have seen success with kale, broccoli, and radishes in shaded areas.

(14) Patio and balcony gardens also require different containers. (15) Planting directly in the soil is not possible. (16) This means that gardeners may have large pots, raised beds, hanging baskets, window boxes, or even rows of pots or boxes hung on the wall. (17) Depending on the amount of sun and wind, special soils or mulch may be needed to keep plants moist or to keep water from collecting. (18) These soils can be heavy, especially after watering, so gardeners should make sure that any balcony or railing can support the weight before placing pots or boxes. (19) Resin or plastic containers are lighter than ceramic or terra cotta pots. (20) Additionally, containers should be secured to keep them from being knocked down or blown by gusts.

(21) Some gardeners may prefer a practical vegetable garden or rows of herbs. (22) Others decorate their small garden spaces with a multitude of flowers that look and smell beautiful. (23) A gardener's personality can be seen in the type of garden he or she chooses to grow. (24) Whether a gardener wants to grow fruit, vegetables, flowers, or just be near shades of green, there are plenty of options. (25) In an area with enough sunlight, a bit of soil, and a few containers, a miniature paradise can be created.

30. Sentence 4 is not an effective topic sentence for paragraph 2. Which of the following sentences should be used in place of sentence 4?

a. The first thing to consider is sunlight.
b. Plants can grow well in different areas.
c. The Sun shines on gardens, balconies, and patios.
d. Photosynthesis depends on the Sun.

31. Sentences 5 and 6 should be combined. Use the lines below to write a new sentence that includes the information given in sentences 5 and 6.

____

____

____

32. Which of the following sentences should be removed from paragraph 2?

a. Sentence 7
b. Sentence 9
c. Sentence 10
d. Sentence 13

33. Which of the following sentences should be added after sentence 25 to improve this essay's conclusion?

a. Gardeners must simply remember to consider the sunlight, soil, and space in which they plant their garden.
b. There are many different reasons to start a garden, as well as endless ways to create a successful one.
c. Different plants respond well to different conditions, so gardeners should carefully plan their gardens.
d. The only thing that limits an aspiring gardener with a small space is the extent of his or her imagination.

Editing

Kelsey is writing an essay about worms. Read the following paragraphs from the body of her essay and look for errors that Kelsey needs to correct. Once you have read the paragraphs, answer the questions that follow them.

All About Worms

(1) Worms like night crawlers and earthworms help keep soil healthy by moving organic matter from the surface down into the soil. (2) Eventually, a tree leaf can take three to five years to decompose and be incorporated into the soil. (3) In forests infested with night crawlurs, this process can take as little as four weeks! (4) By speeding up the breakdown of plant material, earthworms also speed up the rate at which nutrients are precycled back to the plants.

(5) Worms and other soil organisms are a more necessary part of the soil food web. (6) Without them, all the organic matter would build up on the soil surface and never get down into the soil. (7) To grow healthy, productive plants, you need healthy, productive soil. (8) Organisms in the soil provide food for plants when they need it and in a form they can use.

34. Which change would correct the mistake in sentence 2?

a. Change *Eventually* to *Normally.*
b. Add a comma after *leaf.*
c. Change *to* to *too.*
d. Change *be* to *been.*

35. Which change would correct the mistake in sentence 3?

a. Change *In* to *On.*
b. Change *crawlurs* to *crawlers.*
c. Change *take* to *took.*
d. Change *four* to *for.*

36. Which word should be used in place of precycled in sentence 4?

By speeding up the breakdown of plant material, earthworms also speed up the rate at which nutrients are __________back to the plants.

decycled
recycled
incycled
upcycled

37. Which change would correct the mistake in sentence 5?

a. Add a comma after *Worms.*
b. Change *are* to *is.*
c. Change *more necessary* to *necessary.*
d. No change is needed in sentence 5.

Gina is writing a narrative essay about a boy named Hobie. Read the following paragraph from the body of her essay and look for errors that Gina needs to correct. Once you have read the paragraph, answer the questions that follow.

Hobie's Big Race

(1) Hobie felt his legs fly through the air and his chest started to hurt a little. (2) He puffed his cheeks and swung his arms hard. (3) Two more laps to go. (4) Hobie kept pace a few feet behind the runner in the lead until they rounded the last bend of the track. (5) Hobie drew a deep, ragged breath and started to run a little faster, making the distance between him and the other runner a few feet shorter. (6) Hobie kept sprinting until he was running side by side with the runner in the lead. (7) The finish line came into view, and he could hear his families cheering for him. (8) His older brother called out, Come on, Hobie! You can do it! (9) With his last ounce of strength, Hobie pushed past the other runner and swung his arms as hard as he could. (10) He flyed over the finish line four yards ahead of the other runner.

38. Which change would correct the mistake in sentence 1?

a. Change *his* to *him.*
b. Change *through* to *with.*
c. Add a comma after *air.*
d. Change *hurt* to *hert.*

39. Which change would correct the mistake in sentence 7?

a. Change *finish line* to *Finish Line.*
b. Change *came* to *comes.*
c. Change *hear* to *here.*
d. Change *families* to *family.*

40. Which change would correct the mistake in sentence 8?

a. Change *called* to *calling.*
b. Add quotation marks before *Come* and after *it!*
c. Change *Come* to *come.*
d. No change is needed in sentence 8.

41. Which change would correct the mistake in sentence 10?

a. Change *flyed* to *flew.*
b. Change *four* to *for.*
c. Add a comma after *yards.*
d. Change *the other runner* to *an other runner.*

Answer Key and Explanations for Test #1

Reading

1. A: TEKS Standard (5.3)(B)

The word *absorb* means to soak up. When water is poured onto normal wood, the wood will soak in the water, so choice A is correct. Wood that has recently absorbed water may look darker. However, the color will eventually return to the way it was, even if there is still water in the wood. Becoming darker is one possible effect of water being absorbed, but it is not the meaning of *absorb*, so choice B is incorrect. Pouring water on wood does not cause the wood to push water away, so choice C is incorrect. The passage explains that absorbing water is different from making things stick together through cohesion, so choice D is incorrect.

2. A: TEKS Standard (5.7)(C)

This sentence shows that water is different from glue because it explains that water will not harden to make things stick together. This sentence contrasts the description of how glue holds things together in paragraph 3. Choice B is a sentence from the experiment. This sentence does not compare water to glue or contrast the behavior of water and glue, so it is incorrect. Choice C describes how water's atoms stick together. However, the way that glue's atoms stick together is not described in the passage. While this sentence describes a quality of water, it does not contrast it with the qualities of glue, so choice C is incorrect. Choice D explains which atoms water is made of, but it does not describe the performance or function of water, so it is incorrect.

3. D: TEKS Standard (5.6)(G)

Paragraph 3 explains that glue is sticky in two ways: through adhesion and cohesion. This supports the key idea that there are multiple ways for a substance to be sticky, so choice D is correct. This idea is also supported by the passage overall, since it is about the unexpected way that water can be sticky. Paragraph 3 does not include information about whether glue is solid or liquid, so choice A is incorrect. Paragraph 3 only talks about glue. It does not talk about the chemical properties of water, so choice B is incorrect. Paragraph 3 does not talk about the purpose of water, so choice C is incorrect.

4. C: TEKS Standard (5.6)(H)

The experiment instructions caution readers against throwing pennies in. The instructions say to slip the pennies in gently and avoid creating a splash, so the reader can conclude that splashing could affect the results of the experiment. The reader cannot conclude that other liquids would behave in the same way as water, especially because water is described as a unique substance in paragraph 4, so choice A is incorrect. The reader cannot conclude that the same number of pennies will make the water spill each time. The experiment directions say that usually it takes more than 10 pennies, and that a scientist was able to put in 25 pennies. This shows the reader that the number of pennies that result in a spill may vary, so choice B is incorrect. Glue and water are described in paragraph 2 as being sticky in different ways. The passage also does not suggest that glue and water are similar, so the reader cannot conclude that glue is made of the same elements as water. This makes choice D incorrect.

5. D: TEKS Standard (5.9)(Di)

The passage first describes the properties of water and then describes an experiment that demonstrates the stickiness of water. Someone would not normally expect water, which we encounter in our everyday lives, to be sticky. However, the information in the passage and shows why water can be considered sticky. The passage does not describe multiple science experiments or explain how safe they are, so choice A is incorrect. The main idea of the passage is about water, not glue. Glue is simply used as an example that is compared to water, so choice B is incorrect. Water being used to wash away stickiness does show water's qualities, but the use of water to wash things is not the main idea of the passage, so choice C is incorrect.

6. C: TEKS Standard (5.9)(Diii)

Paragraphs 3 and 4 show that water and glue are sticky in different ways by comparing their qualities. Paragraphs 3 and 4 do not describe different uses for water, so choice A is incorrect. Paragraphs 3 and 4 do not describe what to do with water in the experiment. That information is given later in the passage, so choice B is incorrect. Water's washing qualities are mentioned in the first paragraph. The purpose of this passage is to inform, not persuade. Additionally, this information does help the reader understand that water itself is sticky, so choice D is incorrect.

7. C: TEKS Standard (5.10)(A)

The author explains the sticky qualities of water by defining cohesion. The author also provides instructions for an experiment that show how water will stick to itself. This shows that choice C is correct. The passage does not provide a sequence of events or explain how the stickiness of water was discovered, so choice A is incorrect. The passage is not written in order to argue that water is the most unique substance. The passage includes facts that make water unique, but this is not the main topic of the passage, so choice B is incorrect. The passage does not contain information about other experiments, so choice D is incorrect.

8. B: TEKS Standard (5.6)(F)

The section explains that when each penny is added to the water, the water molecules pack together and hold on to each other because of cohesion. This happens because of the water's properties, so it is not caused by the pennies. This supports the inference that the experiment could be done with other small objects. This section does not discuss glue or suggest that glue does not have cohesion, which makes choice A incorrect. This section says that the experiment can be done more than once. It also says that the number of pennies that can be added is not always the same. This describes the same experiment, but does not introduce other experiments, so choice C is incorrect. In paragraph 3, the properties of cohesion and adhesion are explained as two different things, not the same thing. Additionally, this section does not mention adhesion, so choice D is incorrect.

9. B: TEKS Standard (5.10)(Dii)

The bullet points list the four items needed to complete the experiment. This list helps the reader understand what they will need to gather before starting the experiment. The text after each bullet point names an item needed for the experiment, but it does not tell the reader how to use the item. The text does not provide step-by-step instructions, so choice A is incorrect. The text in the list does not include similes that help the reader understand how molecules look, so choice C is incorrect. The information in the list does not show how safe or easy the experiment is, as the list only contains the supplies that are needed for the experiment. The list does not describe the actual experiment, so choice D is incorrect.

10. D: TEKS Standard (5.6)(G)

The speaker describes that his shadow "sometimes shoots up taller" and "sometimes gets so little." The speaker, a child, also states that the shadow does not grow "like proper children." These descriptions of the shadow show that it is not always the same size as the speaker, so choice D is incorrect. The shadow changes sizes, but the poem does not suggest that the shadow is doing this in order to tease the speaker. The shadow's motivation for changing size is not mentioned at all, so choice A is incorrect. The fact that the speaker's shadow can only being seen in the daylight is best supported later in the poem. Lines 13-16 support this by explaining that the shadow was not present in the early morning before the Sun came up. Choice B is incorrect. The speaker says that the way his shadow shrinks and grows is funny. However, the speaker does not suggest that the shadow is doing this on purpose or trying to be funny. These lines do not show that the speaker thinks the shadow is being silly, so choice C is incorrect.

11. C: TEKS Standard (5.9)(B)

Personification means describing something with human-like qualities. In lines 9 through 12, the speaker says that the shadow does not know how to play, embarrasses the speaker with its actions, and is a "coward" because it wants to stay close to the speaker. These lines show that the shadow is making choices that the speaker does not like. The shadow would not do these things if the speaker controlled it. This personification suggests that the shadow makes its own decisions with its own mind, so choice C is correct. These lines do not suggest that the shadow does not like the speaker, since the shadow's motivation is not explained. Choice A is incorrect. The shadow does not speak or communicate in the poem, so choice B is incorrect. Since the shadow's reason for making a fool of the speaker is not explained, the poem does not support the idea that the shadow is playing tricks. Choice D is incorrect.

12. B, E: TEKS Standard (5.6)(F)

Even though the shadow is not a living thing, the speaker describes his shadow as if it behaves like a person. The speaker questions some of the shadow's actions, such as how it grows and sticks to him. The speaker also criticizes these actions, calling the shadow a coward and saying that he is not like "proper children." The reader can conclude that the speaker does not understand why his shadow behaves the way it does, so choice B is correct. Choice E is correct because the speaker calls the shadow a coward and says that it is lazy. The speaker does not suggest that he wants to befriend his shadow. In fact, the speaker complains that the shadow makes a "fool" of him, so choice A is incorrect. The speaker does not seem to worry that the shadow is lonely. Instead, the speaker calls the shadow a "coward" for sticking so closely with him all the time, so choice C is incorrect. The speaker suggests that the shadow is scared in line 11, and he does not mention being scared of the shadow, so choice D is incorrect.

13. D: TEKS Standard (5.7)(C)

This choice describes the shadow completing an action in the same way and at the same time as the speaker. Choice D is correct. In choice A, the speaker notes the shadow's behavior, but this does not describe how the shadow moves. This makes choice A incorrect. In choice B, the shadow "stayed behind" when the speaker got up, so the shadow did not move with the speaker. This makes choice B incorrect. Choice C describes how the shadow can suddenly grow, but not how it moves with the speaker, so it is incorrect.

14. A: TEKS Standard (5.10)(D)

The simile "like an India-rubber ball" is used to help the reader imagine how quickly the shadow's height increases. The shadow in the poem quickly "shoots up taller," just like a toy bouncy ball can shoot up quickly when it is bounced. The simile compares the shadow to a ball's fast movement, not a ball's round shape, so choice B is incorrect. The speaker is comparing the shadow to the ball in order to describe the shadow. The speaker is not expressing a hope that he has for the shadow, so choice C is incorrect. The simile does not demonstrate that shadows can be tinier than a toy ball because it is used to describe how the shadow "shoots up taller" and grows. Choice D is incorrect.

15. C: TEKS Standard (5.6)(H)

In lines 13-16, the speaker went out "before the sun was up," but his shadow "stayed at home" and "was fast asleep in bed." The speaker was up and moving, but his shadow was not with him. Shadows are created when something gets in the way of a shining light. Based on the lines in the poem and this fact about shadows, the reader can infer that the speaker's shadow cannot be seen without light. Choice C is correct. Lines 13-16 describe a time when the speaker could not see his shadow, so the reader cannot infer that the shadow can be seen at any time of day or night. This makes choice A incorrect. These lines do not describe the shadow's emotions or suggest that the shadow was upset, so choice B is incorrect. The poem does not suggest that the speaker enjoys his shadow. Additionally, the speaker calls the shadow "lazy" in line 15, which is not the same as "boring." Choice D is incorrect.

16. B: TEKS Standard (5.3)(C)

The word *downtrodden* uses the prefix *down-*. It also includes the word *trodden*, which comes from the root word *tread*. This word means that something has been exhausted, walked over, or worn out. Something treated in this manner would have a distressed appearance, so choice B is correct. Other words in the paragraph support this idea by explaining that the neighborhood looks dusty and old. Choice A is incorrect because the word is used to describe the appearance of the neighborhood. The neighborhood's appearance does not show whether or not it is an unhappy place to live. In fact, paragraph 4 says that Manolo and Barry love living in it. Choice C is incorrect as *downtrodden* is used to describe the landscape, not the walking paths. Choice D is incorrect as the word *downtrodden* does not refer to where a place is located.

17. D: TEKS Standard (5.10)(E)

In a third-person omniscient point of view, the narrator knows the feelings and thoughts of more than one character. In paragraph 4, the narrator describes Barry and Manolo's feelings about living in their neighborhood. Additionally, in paragraph 20, the narrator shows that Barry, Manolo, and Mrs. Juarez are looking forward to starting the new gardens. This shows that choice D is correct. Choice A only provides facts about one of the story's characters (Mrs. Juarez) without knowledge of her thoughts or feelings, so it is incorrect. Choice B does not show any knowledge of thoughts or feelings of the story's characters, so it is incorrect. Choice C only demonstrates knowledge of Mrs. Juarez's thoughts, so it is incorrect.

18. A: TEKS Standard (5.8)(A)

Just before this event, in paragraph 9, Barry and Manolo are surprised to see healthy plants growing in their neighborhood. Mrs. Juarez explains how this is possible, and the boys learn that it is possible for plants to grow well in the desert. This supports the theme that the unexpected is possible, so choice A is correct. While Mrs. Juarez and the boys show each other generosity in paragraphs 13 through 20, these events are minor details in the story. The impact of their generosity is not shown in the passage, so choice B is incorrect. Barry and Manolo's friendship is not described or discussed in the passage, so choice C is incorrect. The passage does not show Barry and Manolo overcoming a challenge through teamwork, so choice D is also incorrect.

19. C: TEKS Standard (5.8)(B)

Barry and Manolo both happily accept the plants Mrs. Juarez offered them, and they are eager to plant them. They thank her for the plants, and these events show that they are grateful to Mrs. Juarez for giving them the plants. This means that choice C is correct. While Barry does think about how it would hurt to run into a cactus, he does not show concern for Mrs. Juarez, which makes choice A incorrect. Barry and Manolo's behavior does not show that they are frustrated. In fact, after meeting Mrs. Juarez, they are excited to change their plans and take their plants home, so choice B is incorrect. As the story ends, Barry and Manolo are eager to put their new plants from Mrs. Juarez into their own gardens, not to show her the playground, so choice D is incorrect.

20. D: TEKS Standard (5.10)(A)

The passage describes events from history in the order that they happened. These events resulted in the creation of three mountain carvings in America. The passage describes the creation of other mountain carvings besides the Crazy Horse Memorial, so choice A is incorrect. The passage does not describe what the artists thought and felt as they created the carvings, so choice B is incorrect. The passage gives facts about each mountain carving sculpture. These facts are not used to try to convince the reader to make their sculpture, so choice C is incorrect.

21. A: TEKS Standard (5.10)(C)

The photograph allows the reader to see what each president looks like in the Mount Rushmore carving. Because the photograph is included, the reader can clearly see what Borglum's carving looks like. The picture does not show Gutzon Borglum's other mountain carvings, so the reader cannot compare them to the Mount Rushmore carving. This means that choice B is incorrect. The picture does not show any of the techniques used by the artist to carve Mount Rushmore, so choice C is incorrect. The picture shows only the finished product of Mount Rushmore. It does not show the step-by-step process of its carving, so choice D is incorrect.

22. TEKS Standard (5.6)(E)

Part A: C: Both Mrs. Juarez and Gutzon Borglum thought outside the box to make their creations. Mrs. Juarez specifically used plants that can survive in the desert to make her garden. Gutzon Borglum used the side of a mountain to make his carvings. Mrs. Juarez's garden caught the attention of Barry and Manolo, and Borglum's carvings still attract visitors today, so choice C is correct. While both of their creations can be described as beautiful, Mrs. Juarez uses plants and not sculpture, so choice A is incorrect. Mrs. Juarez does not suggest that she wants people to come and see her garden, so choice B is incorrect. It is clear that Gutzon Borglum worked for many years on his large-scale sculptures. However, in "A Garden in the Desert," Mrs Juarez has only lived in the boys' neighborhood for a few weeks. This means that she could have only spent a few weeks on her garden at most, so choice D is incorrect.

Part B: B: The sentence in choice B shows that Mrs. Juarez used creativity and research to find plants that she could add to her yard. Choice A is incorrect because, in this line, Mrs. Juarez is simply telling the boys what a drought-resistant plant is. This line of dialogue does not show Mrs. Juarez's qualities. Choice C simply describes the yard. Although it describes Mrs. Juarez's eye-catching creation, it does not show her creativity, so choice C is incorrect. Choice D is incorrect because it does not describe Mrs. Juarez's yard or show her creativity.

23. D: TEKS Standard (5.6)(E)

Barry and Manolo were able to take Mrs. Juarez's extra plants for their own gardens and plant them with Mrs. Juarez's help. Since they only took the plants with them from Mrs. Juarez's house, they must have been able to make their own gardens with common tools. However, Gutzon Borglum required special skills and tools, like a giant lantern projector, to create a mountain sculpture. In "A Garden in the Desert," Mrs. Juarez specifically mentions that her plants were chosen because they don't need much water, so choice A is incorrect. Neither story gives the reader details about the cost of the garden or the sculptures. The stories also do not say whether or not the creators were concerned about the cost, so choice B is incorrect. Choice C is incorrect because Gutzon Borglum did have help with his sculptures, since the passage notes he had an assistant on the Mount Rushmore project.

24. B: TEKS Standard (5.6)(E)

Both Mrs. Juarez and Gutzon Borglum create art in unexpected places. Mrs. Juarez created a beautiful garden in the desert by thinking creatively and finding the right plants. Gutzon Borglum created a magnificent sculpture from the side of a mountain. Both stories demonstrate the idea in choice B, so it is correct. Friendship is not discussed in "An Artist Thinking BIG," so choice A is incorrect. While Mrs. Juarez is like a mentor to Barry and Manolo, the story does not describe whether or not the boys' gardens were successful or beautiful. "A Garden in the Desert" does not support choice C, so it is incorrect. Choice D is incorrect because both passages describe a landscape being changed. Mrs. Juarez buys and plants vegetation that will look nice. This does not suggest that the landscape was beautiful before. Gutzon Borglum and the other sculptors carved images into mountains. They changed the landscape to create something beautiful, but the passage does not say that the landscape was beautiful without the sculptures.

Extended Response

25. TEKS Standard (5.7)(B)

Please use the rubric below to make sure your response meets these criteria. Try to have a friend or family member grade your response for you or take a break after writing your response and return to grade it yourself with fresh eyes.

Below is an excerpt of the STAAR Grades 3-5 Informational Writing Rubric.

Score Point	Organization and Development of Ideas
3	• **Central idea is clear and fully developed** The central idea is clearly identifiable. The focus is consistent throughout, creating a response that is unified and easy to follow. • **Organization is effective** A purposeful structure that includes an effective introduction and conclusion is evident. The organizational structure is appropriate and effectively supports the development of the central idea. The sentences, paragraphs, or ideas are logically connected in purposeful and highly effective ways. • **Evidence is specific, well chosen, and relevant** The response includes relevant text-based evidence that is clearly explained and consistently supports and develops the central idea. For pairs in grades 3-5, evidence is drawn from at least one text. The response reflects a thorough understanding of the writing purpose. • **Expression of ideas is clear and effective** The writer's word choice is specific, purposeful, and enhances the response. Almost all sentences and phrases are effectively crafted to convey the writer's ideas and contribute to the overall quality of the response and the clarity of the message.
Score Point	**Conventions**
2	Student writing demonstrates **consistent command** of grade-level-appropriate conventions, including correct: • sentence construction • punctuation • capitalization • grammar • spelling The response has few errors, but those errors do not impact the clarity of the writing.

Revising

26. B: TEKS Standard (5.11)(Bi)

Sentence 6 describes what Simon did during the time Pedro was gone. Pedro got his money at the same time that Simon was looking at the plane. The transition at the beginning of sentence 6 should show this relationship. Choice B is correct because it means that the events were happening at the same time. Choice A is incorrect because it would mean that Simon looked at the plane until Pedro left to get his money. This is not true because Simon looked at the plane after Pedro left. Choice C is incorrect because it would mean that Pedro getting his money is the reason that Simon began looking at the plane. The passage does not support this idea. Choice D is incorrect because it suggests that it is unclear whether or not Pedro was getting his money. The passage confirms that he was, so *whether* is not a good choice for this sentence.

27. C: TEKS Standard (5.11)(Bii)

Choice C shows why Pedro was helping Simon after Simon told his father that he did not want help. The sentence in choice C shows that Simon changed his mind and realized that Pedro's help would be a good thing to have. Choice A is incorrect because Simon's father is the one that taught him how to build models. Simon knows that his father can help him. Choice B is incorrect because Simon later states in sentence 23 that he asked Pedro to help him. Additionally, the story does not show that Pedro had gotten upset. Choice D is incorrect because Simon has built models before and knows how difficult it can be. The story does not support the idea that Simon would listen to Pedro over his father.

28. C: TEKS Standard (5.11)(C)

Sentence 31 does not present information in a logical order. Choice C clearly states the information in an order that makes sense and is easy to read. Choices A and B are incorrect because they are not clear or easy to understand. Choice D is incorrect because it changes the meaning of the sentence. Choice C suggests that Simon remembered his father's teaching as he and Pedro built the plane, and that it helped him. However, choice D suggests that Simon and Pedro had already made progress on the plane before Simon remembered what his father had taught him. It also does not present information in the most logical order.

29. Traffic: TEKS Standard (5.11)(C)

In sentence 34, Simon's father offers to drive the boys to the store. In sentence 36, Simon confirms what his father said in sentence 35 by saying that traffic has probably gotten worse. This shows that Simon's father is talking about traffic in sentence 35. The other answers are not logical. Simon's father says "It is pretty heavy this time of day," so the time affects how heavy the subject is. Planes, models, and money do not become heavier with time. The time does not change their weight or make more of them appear, so these answer choices are incorrect.

30. A: TEKS Standard (5.11)(Bi)

Sentence 4 is not effective because it does not give the reader any information or show what the topic of the paragraph is. The purpose of paragraph 2 is to tell gardeners that they should consider the amount of sunlight that plants need. Choice A states this and gives the reader a better idea of the topic of the paragraph. Choice A is correct. Choice B is incorrect because this information has already been given in sentence 3. This sentence also does not tell the reader what the paragraph is about. Choice C is incorrect because it does not provide needed information. The reader knows that the Sun can shine in different places. This sentence also does not connect sunlight to gardening, it simply states that the Sun shines on gardens. Choice A, however, shows that gardeners need to think about sunlight when planning their gardens. Choice D is incorrect because this information is stated in sentence 5 and does not show the topic of the paragraph.

31. TEKS Standard (5.11)(C)

The new sentence should include the information given in lines 5 and 6. The sentence should be similar to the following sentence: Plants need the Sun to perform photosynthesis, but some plants need more than others. This sentence includes the fact that plants need the Sun for photosynthesis and the fact that not all plants need the same amount of sunlight. The sentence should also be complete, grammatically correct, and clear.

32. C: TEKS Standard (5.11)(Bii)

Sentence 10 should be removed because it does not support the paragraph and is not needed. Paragraph 2 is about the amount of sunlight that different plants need. Sentence 10 simply states that some plants cannot live in patio and balcony gardens. This does not help the reader understand the topic of the paragraph or the other information given, so choice C is correct. Choice A is incorrect because this sentence gives examples of different areas with different sunlight and supports the information in sentences 5 and 6. Choice B is incorrect because sentence 9 gives examples of plants that can live in partial shade. This supports the information in sentence 8. Choice D is incorrect because it provides information that supports the paragraph and helps the reader understand the information that is given.

33. D: TEKS Standard (5.11)(Bi)

The concluding sentence should be related to the overall topic of the passage. It should also give the reader a sense that the passage has reached its end. The concluding sentence should not focus on one small detail or state any information that was not given somewhere else in the passage. Choice D is the best choice because it relates to the overall topic of the passage, which is gardening with a small space. It also summarizes the ideas in the passage by suggesting that there are many ways to create a garden in a small space. Choice A is incorrect because it does not relate to the topic of small gardens. It also simply restates the topic of each body paragraph. Choice B is incorrect because it is not related to the topic of the passage. Choice C is incorrect because it focuses on small details instead of the overall topic.

Editing

34. A: TEKS Standard (5.11)(Dv)

The word *eventually* does not fit at the beginning of this sentence. Sentence 2 is describing how long most tree leaves take to decompose. Since this sentence is not describing one event, *eventually* should not be used here. *Normally* should be used, since it shows that the sentence is talking about a process that happens often and can happen differently. Choice A is correct. There is no need to add a comma after *leaf*, so choice B is incorrect. The word *to* is a preposition, and the word *too* is a synonym of *also*. In sentence 2, the word *to* is used as a preposition, so it is spelled correctly, and choice C is incorrect. *Be* is a present-tense verb, and *been* is a past-tense verb. Sentence 2 is in the present tense, so it should use present-tense verbs. *Be* is used correctly in sentence 2, so choice D is incorrect.

35. B: TEKS Standard (5.2)(Bi)

The word *crawlers* is spelled using the suffixes *-er* and *-s*. In sentence 3, it is misspelled as *crawlurs*, so choice B is correct. The process of leaves decaying takes place within a forest, not on top of or over the forest, so choice A is incorrect. *Take* is a present-tense verb, and *took* is a past-tense verb. Sentence 3 is in present tense, so the verb *take* is used correctly and choice C is incorrect. The word *four* is a number and the word *for* is a preposition. In sentence 3, the word *four* is used to show how many weeks it may take for a leaf to decay. *Four* is spelled correctly, so choice D is incorrect.

36. recycled: TEKS Standard (5.2)(Bv)

The prefix *pre-* means something happens before something else. The prefix *re-* means that something happens again. This sentence says that the nutrients are going through a process that puts them into plants again. This shows that the word that goes in the blank should show something happening again. Since the prefix *re-* means "happening again," *recycled* is the correct word. *De-* means that something is removed or undone. *In-* means that one thing is within another, or that one thing is the opposite of another. The word *upcycled* means that parts of objects are put together to create something new. *Incycled*, *decycled*, and *upcycled* do not fit the meaning of this sentence, so they are all incorrect.

37. C: TEKS Standard (5.11)(Div)

Comparative adjectives are used when comparing two things, and they usually end in the suffix *-er* or are used with the word *more*. Standard adjectives are used to describe just one thing. In this sentence, the word *necessary* is used to describe one group of organisms. As written, it is used with the word *more*, so it is used as a comparative adjective. Since *necessary* only describes one thing, it should be a standard adjective. *More* should be removed from the sentence, so choice C is correct. *Worms* is an item in a list of only two items, so no comma is needed and choice A is incorrect. *Are* is a plural verb, and *is* is a singular verb. The word *are* follows the noun *organisms*, which is plural. Since *organisms* is plural, it should be used with a plural verb like *are*, so choice B is incorrect. Choice D is incorrect since *more* needs to be removed from the sentence.

38. C: TEKS Standard (5.11)(Di)

Sentence 1 is written using two independent clauses. Independent clauses should be joined by either a semicolon or a comma followed by a coordinating conjunction. Sentence 1 includes two independent clauses and a coordinating conjunction, but no comma. A comma should be added after *air*, so choice C is correct. *His* is a possessive pronoun, and *him* is an objective pronoun. *His* is used in sentence 1 to show that the sentence is talking about the legs and chest belonging to Hobie. A possessive pronoun is the correct type of pronoun to use in sentence 1, so choice A is incorrect. Sentence 1 says "Hobie felt his legs fly through the air." The preposition *with* is used to show that two nouns are completing an action together or that two events are happening at the same time. Hobie's legs are flying, but the air is not flying with them. *Through* is the right preposition to use in this clause, so choice B is incorrect. *Hurt* is spelled with a *u*, not an *e*, so choice D is incorrect.

39. D: TEKS Standard (5.11)(Diii)

The word *family* is a collective noun that is used instead of naming the members of the family. Even though *family* represents multiple people, it is a singular noun. *Families* is the plural form of *family*. Only one family is mentioned in sentence 7, so choice D is correct. The finish line in this story is not a proper noun, so choice A is incorrect. Sentence 7 is written in the past tense. *Came* is a past-tense verb, and *comes* is a present-tense verb. *Came* is used correctly in sentence 7, so choice B is incorrect. *Hear* means that someone can detect a sound. *Here* is used instead of naming a specific place. In sentence 7, Hobie can detect the sound of his family cheering for him, so *hear* is the correct word to use. Choice C is incorrect.

40. B: TEKS Standard (5.11)(Dx)

Dialogue, or words spoken by a character, should include quotation marks. The quotation marks should be placed before the first word in the dialogue and after the last word in the dialogue. Hobie's brother's dialogue begins with *Come* and ends with *it!*, so choice B is correct. *Called* is a past-tense verb, and *calling* is a present-tense verb. Since sentence 8 is written in the past tense, *called* is used correctly, and choice A is incorrect. When dialogue starts with a new sentence, the first word in the dialogue should be capitalized. Hobie's brother's dialogue begins with a new sentence, so the first word, *come*, should be capitalized. Choice C is incorrect. Since quotation marks needed to be added to the sentence, choice D is incorrect.

41. A: TEKS Standard (5.11)(Dii)

Fly is an irregular verb because when it is written in past tense, it is not spelled by adding *-ed* to the present-tense form of the verb. In past tense, *fly* becomes *flew*, so choice A is correct. *Four* is a number, and *for* is a preposition. Sentence 10 describes how many yards were between Hobie and the runner behind him. This means that *four*, the number, is used correctly in this sentence, so choice B is incorrect. Commas do not usually need to be added before prepositional phrases, so choice C is incorrect. *The* is a definite article used to point out a specific thing. *An* is an indefinite article used to point out any one of something. The sentence is talking about one specific other runner, so *the* is the correct article to use, and choice D is incorrect.

Practice Test #2

Reading

Little White Lily
by George MacDonald

Little White Lily
Sat by a stone,
Drooping and waiting
Till the sun shone.
Little White Lily
Sunshine has fed;
Little White Lily
Is lifting her head.

Little White Lily
Said: "It is good
Little White Lily's
Clothing and food."
Little White Lily
Dressed like a bride!
Shining with
whiteness,
And crownèd beside!

Little White Lily
Drooping with pain,
Waiting and waiting
For the wet rain.
Little White Lily
Holdeth her cup;
Rain is fast falling
And filling it up.

Little White Lily
Said: "Good again,
When I am thirsty
To have the nice rain.
Now I am stronger,
Now I am cool;
Heat cannot burn me,
My veins are so full."

Little White Lily
Smells very sweet;
On her head sunshine,
Rain at her feet.
Thanks to the
sunshine,
Thanks to the rain,
Little White Lily
Is happy again.

Jack's First Christmas in Africa

(1) "Hi, Jack," said Mom. "How was your day?"

(2) "Fine, I guess," sighed ten-year-old Jack.

(3) "Is everything all right? You don't sound very convincing."

(4) "Yes, Mom, everything's fine."

(5) Really, though, Jack wasn't fine. He was homesick. He and his parents had moved to Africa six months earlier to be missionaries. Africa was very different than America, but most of the time Jack was happy. He had made friends at the school, he was getting used to the bizarre food, and even living in a hut had become enjoyable. But now it was close to Christmas, and Jack missed America more than ever.

(6) Some of the African people didn't even celebrate Christmas, and the ones who did had very different traditions. There were no authentic Christmas trees, no ornaments, and definitely no snow. He wouldn't be enjoying any of his mom's special Christmas cookies because there was no way to get the ingredients needed to bake them. And just what kind of present did Jack expect to get? No new video games, no new skateboard, no new toys at all. None of these things were available in the little village in the middle of the African jungle.

(7) Then, one day at school, their class began talking about Christmas.

(8) "Tell us, Jack. How do you celebrate Christmas in America?" said Wahid.

(9) "Well, first we put up a Christmas tree in our home."

(10) "A Christmas tree?" asked Jalil. "I have never heard of such a thing."

(11) "It's an evergreen tree, one that never loses its leaves. We hang all sorts of decorations all over it, even lights," said Jack.

(12) Jack's classmates listened in amazement to all that Jack had to share about Christmas in America. He told them about all the great food they ate and wrapping presents for his parents in beautiful red, green, silver, and gold paper. He told them about all the family get-togethers, the caroling on the cold winter nights, and the stockings filled with candy and all kinds of treats. He even told them about the special candlelight service they always attended on Christmas Eve.

(13) "Christmas is really about giving, and spending time with friends and family," said Jack.

(14) Finally, a week later, it was the last day of school before the Christmas holidays would start. Jack moved extra slow when he awoke, wishing more than ever he could just stay in his bed. He didn't want to celebrate Christmas in Africa. It just wasn't the same. He dreaded going to school, but he knew he had no choice.

(15) When Jack walked into his classroom, he couldn't believe his eyes. There before him was a Christmas tree! It wasn't the kind of tree he had in America, but it was a tree, and it was covered in decorations, homemade versions of the ones Jack had

described to his class. There were presents under the tree, wrapped in paper that had been painted. The colors were red and green with accents of gold and silver. On the table, there were several dozen special African cookies, along with some punch. The students had even cut up tiny pieces of paper and strewn them all over the floor to look like snow.

(16) "Surprise, Jack!" said Wahid. "We wanted to bring American Christmas to you here in Africa."

(17) "Yes," said Jalil. "We know you miss your home, but we are glad you are here to celebrate Christmas with us this year."

(18) "Open your present, Jack," said Ourja.

(19) Jack tore the paper off the present and found a mitt and ball for playing a native African stick game.

(20) Jack smiled. "Thanks, guys," said Jack. "It looks like it's going to be a merry Christmas after all!"

Refer to the passage "Little White Lily" to answer questions 1-3.

1. What can the reader infer based on the poem "Little White Lily"?

a. Lilies always grow by stones.
b. Lilies need to drink water in the evening.
c. Lilies will suffer without sunshine and rain.
d. Lilies are most commonly white.

2. The poet describes the lily as being "dressed like a bride." Why did the poet use this simile?

a. It tells the reader that the lily was feeling nervous and excited.
b. It shows the reader that people were celebrating the lily.
c. It allows the reader to understand that the lily has layers of petals.
d. It helps the reader imagine the lily by comparing it to a wedding dress.

3. In lines 25 through 40, what type of voice does the poet's word choice create?

a. Depressed
b. Thankful
c. Persuasive
d. Silly

Refer to the passage "Jack's First Christmas in Africa" to answer questions 4-8.

4. Read the definitions for *accent* below (adapted from Merriam-Webster).

accent \ ak-sent \ noun
1. a way of speaking typical of a particular group of people 2. a greater stress placed on a musical tone 3. an object used for emphasis as part of a design 4. a special concern or attention

Which definition of *accent* is used in Paragraph 15?

a. Definition 1
b. Definition 2
c. Definition 3
d. Definition 4

5. Based on the events at the end of "Jack's First Christmas in Africa," what is most likely to happen next?

a. Jack will ask his mother to bake her special cookies to give to his classmates.
b. Jack will still dread waking up tomorrow because he is not in America for Christmas.
c. Jack will use his Christmas gift to play the native African stick game with his classmates.
d. Jack will not eat the special African cookies because they are not the ones his mom makes.

6. How does line 13 in "Jack's First Christmas in Africa" show the theme of the story?

a. Jack recognizes that friendship and time with others are more important than traditions.
b. Jack realizes that he can make new friends by sharing common Christmas traditions.
c. Jack decides to use his experiences to help his family adjust to living in a new country.
d. Jack plans to surprise his friends with Christmas cookies to make them happy.

7. How does paragraph 6 impact the plot of "Jack's First Christmas in Africa"?

a. It shows that Jack is eager to see how his classmates celebrate Christmas.
b. It compares Jack's Christmas in Africa and his Christmas in America.
c. It describes how Jack's family supports him when he feels homesick.
d. It explains how Christmas traditions have helped Jack make friends at school.

8. How does the setting of "Jack's First Christmas in Africa" affect the plot of the story?

a. It creates a situation where Jack has to try new foods and live in a new place.
b. It reveals why Jack has been looking forward to celebrating Christmas in Africa.
c. It shows why Jack's family wanted to move to Africa for missionary work.
d. It makes it difficult for Jack to experience his usual Christmas traditions.

Refer to the passages "Little White Lily" and "Jack's First Christmas in Africa" to answer questions 9-11.

9. How is the lily in "Little White Lily" similar to Jack in "Jack's First Christmas in Africa"?

a. Both realize the value of friendship
b. Both were happy to receive something
c. Both were looking forward to a meal
d. Both wanted to receive care from others

10. What is the main difference between the lily in "Little White Lily" and Jack in "Jack's First Christmas in Africa"?

a. The lily was expecting the sunshine and rain, but Jack was not expecting the Christmas celebration he received.
b. The lily was happy to receive sunshine and rain, but Jack was not happy about the Christmas surprise.
c. The lily was happy being by herself, but Jack wanted to make friends.
d. The lily was living in an unfamiliar place, but Jack was living in his childhood home.

11. What theme is found in "Jack's First Christmas in Africa" that is not found in "Little White Lily"?

a. Being happy to receive something
b. Feeling sad because of lacking something
c. Experiencing the kindness of others
d. Overcoming a challenge through hard work

Composting: A Fun and Easy Way to Reduce Trash

(1) When was the last time you tossed something like a banana peel or an apple core into the trash? Maybe it was sometime this past week, or even earlier today. Every year, thousands of tons of food waste like this go into our landfills. However, some of that waste could be reused to feed the soil and grow new plants, and it is easier than you may think! We are talking about composting, which is a way to recycle waste from food and other natural materials by turning it into soil that is full of nutrients.

Getting Started with Compost is Easy

(2) There are many easy ways to start making compost. A successful compost pile should have a mix of wet and dry items, with more dry items than wet items. Examples of wet items are fruit and vegetable scraps and grass clippings. Examples of dry items are twigs and dry leaves. After you start composting, you can have new soil that is full of nutrients in just a few weeks.

(3) Some people like to use a large container or area outside in their yard. Turning the pile every few days will help the items break down and become soil. There are ways to compost inside too. Some people use worms to compost indoors. Worms eat the wet and dry items, so compost can be made faster.

(4) An easy way to start composting for the first time is by using a small bucket or other container outside. Always ask an adult first, since composting can be messy or smelly if it is not done the right way. Also, larger items may need to be chopped into smaller pieces so they break down more easily. There are many resources out there to help make your compost a success.

(5) Even if your family does not have many fruit or vegetable scraps, there are surprising things you can add to your compost pile. If you have a furry pet, pet hair can be composted. (Human hair can be composted as well.) Adding some types of cloth, wood, or paper products, such as dryer lint, wooden popsicle sticks, and shredded newspaper, is also an unexpected way to feed your compost pile.

(6) Before you throw something in the trash, check and see if it can go in your compost pile. While many unexpected items can become compost, it's important to know what not to put in a compost pile. Meat or dairy products can attract animals, and plastic, glass, and metal will not be able to break down in your pile.

Environmental Benefits of Composting

(7) There are many benefits of composting. One benefit is that the soil from compost is full of nutrients. You can use this new soil to start a garden or feed plants that you might be growing already. Plants can grow strong and healthy when they have enough nutrients from the soil.

(8) A second benefit of composting is that it helps save water. When compost is used in soil, like in gardening, the compost allows the soil to hold more water over time. You will not need to water your garden as often when adding compost.

(9) Finally, one of the biggest benefits is that compost reduces the amount of trash that goes into landfills. Families may throw away thousands of pounds of trash each year, and some of that trash could have been turned into compost.

(10) After you start composting, you can have new soil that is full of nutrients in just a few weeks. You can use this new soil to start a garden, feed your plants, or improve the quality of your existing soil. When you compost, you can feel proud that you are helping the environment by turning trash into something useful and reducing the trash you throw away and the water you use.

Refer to the passage "Composting: A Fun and Easy Way to Reduce Trash" to answer questions 12-18.

12. Based on paragraph 5, which two conclusions can the reader make about composting? Select all that may apply.

a. Old clothing can always go in a compost pile.
b. Compost can only be made with scraps from plants.
c. Dog and cat hair can break down into compost.
d. A compost pile should have more wet items than dry items.
e. Some unexpected materials can be composted.

13. What is the most likely reason the author wrote the passage "Composting: A Fun and Easy Way to Reduce Trash"?

a. To persuade the reader to try composting for themselves
b. To inform the reader of the scientific process behind composting
c. To prove to the reader that composting is the best way to reduce trash
d. To tell the reader how composting can be done indoors

14. Which key idea is supported by paragraph 3?

a. Composting can be done indoors or outdoors.
b. Not all items that we might throw away can go into a compost pile.
c. Composting will only work if it is done in a large container.
d. Composting has many benefits to the environment.

15. The author of the passage claims that composting can reduce trash. How does the author support this claim?

a. By providing a chronological observation of a compost pile's progress
b. By describing how the amount of trash in landfills has increased over the years
c. By giving their first-person experience with starting a compost pile at home
d. By estimating how much trash families throw away every year

16. What conclusion can the reader make about composting based on the passage "Composting: A Fun and Easy Way to Reduce Trash"?

a. Compost made from worms has the most nutrients.
b. Compost is better for plants than fertilizer.
c. Composting can save families thousands of gallons of water each year.
d. Composting does not need to cost money.

17. What is the central claim made in "Composting: A Fun and Easy Way to Reduce Trash"?

a. A compost pile works best when it has partial sunlight each day.
b. Composting is a simple way to support the environment.
c. A compost pile must have mostly wet items.
d. Composting outside is easier than composting with worms inside.

18. Which of the following groups is most likely the author's target audience for this passage?

a. People who want to learn more about how plants grow
b. People who want to help preserve the environment
c. People who want to know where to take their recycling
d. People who do not like to take care of their gardens

A Dreamer Named George Lucas

(1) You may not know the name George Lucas, but you probably know the incredible world he created. He is the mastermind behind such beloved heroes as Luke Skywalker, R2-D2, Chewbacca, and Queen Amidala. He also created such dreaded villains as Darth Vader, Boba Fett, and Emperor Palpatine. These are some of the main characters in the wildly popular series of movies called *Star Wars*. And none of these films would exist if not for a young dreamer from Modesto, California.

(2) George Lucas was born on May 14, 1944. As a young man, George loved driving his car around Modesto and dreamed of becoming a racecar driver. However, he became interested in film while studying at junior college. He focused on film while at the University of Southern California School of Cinematic Arts, where he learned the skills that would make him famous.

(3) At the university, George made his first film. It was a science-fiction story called *THX 1138*. A friend of his thought the film was too serious. He challenged George to make a lighthearted comedy. George rose to the challenge by making a movie called *American Graffiti*. The movie was about a group of teenagers who liked nothing better than driving around town in their cars. The story was not very dramatic. The movie studio was concerned that people would not be interested in his film. But audiences related to the funny, likable characters, and the film became a big hit. George's success with *American Graffiti* meant he would be able to make more films.

(4) For his next project, he returned to science fiction. But instead of making another serious, adult film like *THX 1138*, he decided to make one with the lighthearted, fast-paced feel of *American Graffiti*. Once again, the studio executives were worried that audiences would not like George's space adventure. They thought his world of creatures and robots was too strange. Once again, the studio was wrong. Released in 1977, *Star Wars* made more money than any movie before it. George was right again.

(5) George Lucas spent the next few years working on sequels to his big hit. *The Empire Strikes Back* was released in 1980. *Return of the Jedi* followed in 1983. In the meantime, he created a new character, an adventurer named Indiana Jones. Indiana would go on to star in five popular movies of his own. It seemed that George could only have success, but making these films was a lot of hard work. He decided to take some time off from making movies, although he promised fans that there were more stories to tell in the *Star Wars* universe.

(6) Sixteen years later, George Lucas finally returned to the most successful series in movie history. But instead of picking up where *Return of the Jedi* ended, he decided to tell the story of what happened before the first *Star Wars* movie he made. *The Phantom Menace* was released in 1999. Then came *Attack of the Clones* in 2002 and *Revenge of the Sith* in 2005.

(7) When he isn't making blockbusters, George Lucas likes to spend time with his family. He even allowed his three children to appear in his most recent *Star Wars* movies. Who knows what he will dream up next?

Refer to the passage "A Dreamer Named George Lucas" to answer questions 19-25.

19. How did the author organize the information in the passage to describe George Lucas's story?

a. By using a chronological pattern to describe George Lucas's road to success, starting with his first film in college
b. By using a compare-and-contrast pattern to describe the main characters in the *Indiana Jones* and *Star Wars* series
c. By using description to show George Lucas' creative process for thinking up new movie characters
d. By using order of importance to rank George Lucas' movies from most successful to least successful

20. Paragraphs 3 and 4 of "A Dreamer Named George Lucas" support the key idea that:

a. George Lucas had the goal of making movies since his childhood.
b. George Lucas did not like his film *American Graffiti*.
c. George Lucas' success with his first few movies was surprising.
d. George Lucas did not like being challenged when it came to his movie ideas.

21. Which sentence from the passage shows that George Lucas' first *Star Wars* movie was successful?

a. Once again, the studio executives were worried that audiences would not like George's space adventure.
b. Released in 1977, *Star Wars* made more money than any movie before it.
c. He decided to take some time off from making movies, although he promised fans that there were more stories to tell in the *Star Wars* universe.
d. But instead of picking up where *Return of the Jedi* ended, he decided to tell the story of what happened before the first *Star Wars* movie he made.

22. What does the word *lighthearted* mean, as it is used in paragraphs 3 and 4?

a. Fun, entertaining
b. Floating, weightless
c. Bright, colorful
d. Fragile, weak

23. Which of the following is the best summary of "A Dreamer Named George Lucas"?

a. George Lucas was inspired to become a filmmaker in college. Although it was hard work, he was able to make multiple movies within a few years, such as the *Star Wars* series and the *Indiana Jones* series, before taking a break. He made six *Star Wars* movies from 1977 to 2005.
b. George Lucas gave up his dream to be a racecar driver during college. After he made his first movie, a friend challenged him to make lighthearted movies. People did not think he would do well, but he was still able to make six *Star Wars* movies by the end of 2005.
c. George Lucas had creative ideas for movies. He wanted to make some about an adventurer (*Indiana Jones*) and some about space adventures (*Star Wars*). He chose to work on the *Indiana Jones* movies first because he thought they would be a big hit.
d. George Lucas studied film in college, where his comedy film, *American Graffiti*, was unexpectedly a big hit. His next film, *Star Wars*, was also an unlikely success, making more money than any other movie before it. This success led him to create many more well-known movies, such as the *Indiana Jones* movies and others in the *Star Wars* series.

24. What is the central idea of "A Dreamer Named George Lucas"? Write your response on the lines below. Include evidence from the passage in your response.

____

____

____

____

25. What is the most likely reason that the author named specific heroes and villains as film characters at the beginning of the passage, in paragraph 1?

a. To persuade the reader that *Star Wars* is one of the best movies of all time
b. To show the reader that they may already be familiar with George Lucas' creative ideas
c. To provide a sequence of how George Lucas created each of his film characters
d. To reveal the inspirations for some of George Lucas' film characters

Extended Response

Your STAAR test will include the following instructions for your extended response question. The response prompts used here are similar to the prompts you will see on the STAAR test.

26. Read the passage "A Dreamer Named George Lucas." Based on the passage, write a response to the following:

Explain how George Lucas's friend, the studio executives, and the fans impacted the *Star Wars* movies.

Write a well-organized informational composition that uses specific evidence from the passage to support your answer.

Remember to —

- clearly state your central idea
- organize your writing
- develop your ideas in detail
- use evidence from the selection in your response
- use correct spelling, capitalization, punctuation, and grammar

Manage your time carefully so that you can —

- review the selection
- plan your response
- write your response
- revise and edit your response

Revising

Javier wrote the following paper about his favorite author. Read the following paper and note the revisions that Javier should make. Once you have read his paper, answer the questions that follow it.

The Woman Who Made a Wizard

(1) In 1997, a new writer named J. K. Rowling amazed parents and teachers alike by inspiring young people to read. (2) She did this with the help of a young wizard named Harry Potter. (3) Rowling's book, *Harry Potter and the Philosopher's Stone*, was just the first in a series that would capture the world's imagination.

(4) Joanne Rowling was born near Gloucestershire, England, in 1965. (5) Originally, she was not able to get any of her stories published. (6) Then one day while riding a train, she got an idea. (7) She imagined a boy who seemed ordinary in every way. (8) But, little did he know, he had powers that were anything but ordinary. (9) In fact, little Harry Potter had such amazing powers that he was already famous in the world of his fellow wizards. (10) Suddenly, through her writing, Rowling threw this "normal" boy into a series of incredible adventures. (11) He faced all kinds of creatures, villains, and dangerous situations while making some loyal new friends along the way.

(12) This new idea and story became Rowling's first novel. (13) Although it was long, *Harry Potter and the Philosopher's Stone* became a major hit with young readers. (14) Harry did things next and they could not wait to find out what. (15) J. K. Rowling did not make them wait long. (16) She published *Harry Potter and the Chamber of Secrets* just a year after her first book. (17) Once again, the book was a success! (18) Later, Rowling followed the sequel with five more books in the series.

(19) The books became so popular that they were made into movies. (20) The first movie came out before the fifth book had even been published! (21) The film series ended with two movies based on the last one, *Harry Potter and the Deathly Hallows*. (22) While the movies were not perfect adaptations of the books, they introduced new fans to the story of Harry Potter. (23) The movies, like the books, won many awards and earned a large profit.

(24) In 2007, J. K. Rowling published her final Harry Potter book, *Harry Potter and the Deathly Hallows*. (25) By this point, both Harry and the readers who loved him had grown up. (26) Rowling was ready to move on too, announcing plans to not only write more children's books, but ones for adults, as well. (27) No matter what J.K. Rowling does next, she will always have many, many fans grateful that she created the most famous little wizard in modern literature.

27. Which of the following sentences would be an appropriate supporting detail to add after sentence 4?

a. Gloucestershire is located in the southern portion of England.
b. Her first child was born before the first *Harry Potter* book came out.
c. In the 1990s, she was a mother dreaming of a career as a writer.
d. She did not write Harry Potter until she was in her 30s.

28. On the lines below, write a revision of sentence 14 that has a clearer meaning.

____

____

____

29. The transition at the beginning of sentence 18 is not very clear. Which of the following transitions should be used to make the sentence clearer?

a. After that
b. A while later
c. Over the next decade
d. In the future

30. Sentence 21 uses unclear wording. Choose the word that should be used instead of *one*.

a. book
b. movie
c. award
d. author

Giada wrote the following paper about walruses. Read the following paper and note the revisions that Giada should make. Once you have read her paper, answer the questions that follow it.

Walruses

(1) What is the funniest-looking animal on earth? (2) Well, there are a lot of funny-looking animals in the world, but without a doubt, one of the funniest-looking ones is the walrus. (3) They look funny when they're sitting around, they look funny when they're lying down, and they really look funny when they pull themselves out of the water or across the ice, using their long tusks to help them move. (4) In fact, walruses are so funny-looking that they're cute! (5) The walrus's scientific name is *Odobenus*, which is Latin for "tooth walker."

(6) Walruses are between 8 and 12 feet long and can weigh nearly 4,000 pounds. (7) They look like gargantuan balls of blubber with two gigantic teeth! (8) In fact, they really are gargantuan balls of blubber—under their skin is a layer of fat that is almost six inches thick. (9) This fat layer is like having a very thick swimsuit on. (10) It keeps them warm in the extremely frigid water where they obtain their food. (11) Their whiskers also contribute to their funny appearance, but they serve an important purpose: they help the walrus find its food. (12) Their tusks are around three feet long and are used for breaking ice, climbing out of the water, and fighting.

(13) Before, walruses have brown skin. (14) It turns lighter and lighter as they age, and the older ones look almost pink. (15) They usually live to be around 25 years old, but some can reach as old as 30. (16) Their main foods are small sea creatures such as shrimp, crabs, and clams, which they find on the bottom of the sea. (17) They use their whiskers to feel around for food on the seafloor, and they will force creatures out of hiding by spraying a mouthful of water in their direction. (18) They can stay underwater for long periods before coming up for air. (19) They can also float for hours at the surface because they have airbags under their throats.

(20) There aren't many animals that eat walruses, which is a good thing because they are so big that they can't move fast enough to get away from a predator. (21) Polar bears and killer whales will attack walruses, but usually they eat young or injured ones. (22) An adult walrus can fight back hard. (23) Killer whales and polar bears prefer to avoid adult walruses if they can. (24) All in all, walruses have a pretty nice life. (25) They get to spend their days swimming in the ocean or lying in the sun, and they have all the food they want for free. (26) The only things they really have to worry about are killer whales and polar bears. (27) Most animals would love to have such an easy life. (28) So, walruses might be funny-looking, but they're the ones who have the last laugh!

31. One of the sentences in the first paragraph contains unnecessary information and should be removed. Which sentence should be removed?

a. Sentence 1
b. Sentence 2
c. Sentence 3
d. Sentence 5

32. Which sentence should be added before sentence 6 to improve the transition into the second paragraph?

a. Many animals have tusks, but they do not look very funny.
b. Besides being funny-looking, walruses are also huge.
c. While walruses can be cute, they can also be dangerous
d. Some adult walruses look pink instead of brown.

33. A clearer transition is needed at the beginning of sentence 13. Which phrase should be used to replace before?

a. When they are young
b. A little earlier
c. For a while
d. Until it is time

34. Sentences 22 and 23 can be combined. Write a new sentence on the lines below that correctly combines sentences 22 and 23.

____

____

____

Editing

Tanya is writing a personal narrative essay. Read the following paragraphs from the body of her essay and look for errors that Tanya needs to correct. Once you have read the paragraphs, answer the questions that follow them.

Finding Maize

(1) My name is Tanya, and I have a dog whose name is Maize. (2) I found her one summer outside of the supermarket. (3) She were a puppy at the time. (4) I was taking our cart back to the store when I saw a small, black and white animal dart under a row of shopping carts next to the main door. (5) It moved so fast! (6) All I saw was a blur. (7) I did not know if the animal was a cat, a dog, or a skunk until it started barkeeng.

(8) My mom always told me not to play with strange animals, but something about Maize seemed safe. (9) I bent down to look for her under the carts and called to her. (10) She came creepping out, slowly at first. (11) Then she ran straight to me, wagging her tail. (12) I picked her up and brought her back to my mom.

35. Which change would correct the mistake in sentence 3?

a. Change *She* to *Her*.
b. Change *were* to *was*.
c. Add a comma after *puppy*.
d. Change *time* to *tym*.

36. Which change would correct the mistake in sentence 7?

a. Change *did not know* to *did not knew*.
b. Remove the comma after *dog*.
c. Change *barkeeng* to *barking*.
d. No change is needed in sentence 7.

37. Which change would correct the mistake in sentence 10?

a. Change *came* to *come*.
b. Change *creepping* to *creeping*.
c. Change *slowly* to *quickly*.
d. Change *at* to *from*.

Gideon is writing an essay about athlete Roger Staubach. Read the first two paragraphs of his essay and look for errors that Gideon needs to correct. Once you have read the paragraphs, answer the questions that follow them.

Roger Staubach

(1) There are many figures in sports histery that stand out as remarkable, but few can compare to former Dallas Cowboys quarterback Roger Staubach. (2) He was born on February 5, 1942 in Cincinnati, Ohio. (3) Once he attended high school, Staubach enrolled in the United States Naval Academy. (4) As a sophomore in the Naval Academy, Staubach became the Navy's starting quarterback. (5) In his junior year at the Naval Academy, he led the teams to a number-two ranking, losing the Cotton Bowl to number-two-ranked Texas. (6) The Navy's team also defeated Notre Dame, one of their fiercest rivals. (7) That year, Staubach won the Heisman Trophy, which is awarded to the best college football player in America.

(8) Staubach was a 10th-round draft pick of the Dallas Cowboys in the 1964 National Football League (NFL) draft. (9) However, he couldn't start playing professionally right away. (10) As a graduate of the US Naval Academy, he was obligated to serve in the Navy for several years after graduation. (11) Finally, in 1969, he arrived at the Dallas Cowboys training camp just in time to be able to play as a 27-year-old rookie.

38. Which change would correct the mistake in sentence 1?

a. Add a comma after *figures.*
b. Change *histery* to *history.*
c. Change *but* to *and.*
d. Change *Dallas Cowboys* to *Dallas cowboys.*

39. Which word should be used in place of Once in sentence 3?

_______ he attended high school, Staubach enrolled in the United States Naval Academy.

When
As
After
Until

40. Which change would correct the mistake in sentence 5?

a. Change *In* to *Through.*
b. Remove the comma after *Academy.*
c. Change *led* to *leads.*
d. Change *teams* to *team.*

41. Which change would correct the mistake in sentence 9?

a. Change *he* to *him.*
b. Change *couldn't* to *can't.*
c. Change *professionally* to *profeshionally.*
d. No change is needed in sentence 9.

Answer Key and Explanations for Test #2

Reading

1. C: TEKS Standard (5.6)(F)

The poem says that the little white lily droops as it waits for the sunshine and droops in pain as it waits for rain. Once the lily has received both sunshine and rain, the lily "is happy again." While the lily in the poem is sitting by a stone, the poem does not support the idea that all lilies grow by stones. This makes choice A incorrect. The lily receives sunshine before it receives rain. However, the Sun came back out, so the rain did not occur in the evening. Choice B is not supported by the poem, so it is incorrect. The lily in the poem is described as white. However, the poem does not contain information that shows that all lilies are white, so choice D is incorrect.

2. D: TEKS Standard (5.10)(D)

The simile "dressed like a bride" is used to compare the white petals of the lily to a white wedding dress. This comparison helps the reader imagine the color and shape of the lily. Some of the lily's emotions are described in the poem. However, the poem does not include details that show that the lily is excited or nervous, so choice A is incorrect. The poem does not mention people celebrating the lily, so choice B is incorrect. The simile does not provide specific details, such as the number of layers the lily's petals create, so choice C is incorrect.

3. B: TEKS Standard (5.10)(F)

In lines 25 through 40, the lily is thankful for the sunshine and rain after waiting for them. The poet uses specific words to show this. For example, the lily says that the rain makes her "stronger" and "cool" so that she will not burn in the sunlight. In the last stanza, the poet says that "thanks to the sunshine" and "thanks to the rain," the lily is "happy again." This creates a thankful voice, so choice B is correct. These lines do not create a depressed voice because the events being described and the words that are used are positive, so choice A is incorrect. The poem does not attempt to persuade the reader or argue a point, so choice C is incorrect. In lines 25 through 40, the lily is enjoying being saved from a lack of sunshine and rain, which was hurting her. The words used in these lines show that she is happy and thankful because she is no longer in pain. She is not being silly, so choice D is incorrect.

4. C: TEKS Standard (5.3)(A)

In paragraph 15, the presents under the tree for Jack are wrapped in paper that is red and green, "with accents of gold and silver." This description shows that the accents must be things that are added to the red and green paper. Definition 3 describes the way that the gold and silver were used as part of the design of the wrapping paper, so choice C is correct. The word *accent* is not used to describe a way of speaking in the passage, so choice A is incorrect. The author does not use the word *accent* when describing music, so choice B is incorrect. The author does not use the word *accent* when describing a character's concern or attention, so choice D is incorrect.

5. C: TEKS Standard (5.6)(C)

Paragraph 20 shows that Jack has changed his mind about spending Christmas in Africa by the end of the story. He is likely to use his gift, as he is grateful for it and was surprised by the kindness of his classmates. Jack is not likely to ask his mother to bake her special cookies. Paragraph 6 says that there is no way to get the ingredients used to make them, so choice A is incorrect. Jack is not likely to dread Christmas morning in Africa. His classmates have worked hard to cheer him up and help him enjoy being in Africa for Christmas, so choice B is incorrect. The reader can infer that Jack is grateful for the unexpected kindness of his classmates, so Jack is not likely to refuse to eat the cookies his classmates made for him. Choice D is incorrect.

6. A: TEKS Standard (5.8)(A)

In line 13, Jack tells his classmates that Christmas is about giving and spending time with friends and family. The end of the story shows Jack that the kindness of his friends is more valuable than participating in the Christmas traditions he is used to. These ideas support choice A, so it is the correct answer. The passage points out that Jack and his classmates have "very different traditions," so choice B is incorrect. The passage does not show that Jack wants to help his family adjust to living in Africa. The passage only describes how Jack feels about living in Africa, so choice C is incorrect. Jack does not plan a surprise for his classmates. Instead, Jack's classmates surprise him for Christmas, so choice D is incorrect.

7. B: TEKS Standard (5.8)(C)

Paragraph 6 lists the things Jack does not have to celebrate Christmas in Africa that he is used to having in America. This contrast is important to the plot because it shows that Jack does not expect to experience any of his American traditions in Africa. This is the main conflict of the story. The conflict is resolved when Jack's classmates surprise him by recreating the traditions he is used to. Choice B is correct. Paragraph 6 shows what Jack misses about Christmas in America. It does not show that he is eager to see African Christmas traditions, so choice A is incorrect. Paragraph 6 does not describe how Jack's family supports him, so choice C is incorrect. Paragraph 6 does not explain how Jack made friends at school, so choice D is incorrect.

8. D: TEKS Standard (5.8)(D)

The story is set in Africa. Jack is from America, where he got to participate in Christmas traditions that he loved. Africa and America are very different, and the differences make it hard for Jack to participate in the Christmas traditions he enjoys. The passage does show that Jack has gotten used to the food in Africa and their new home. However, these details are not what creates the conflict in the story, so choice A is incorrect. The passage explains that Jack is dreading celebrating Christmas in Africa. He is not looking forward to celebrating it, so choice B is incorrect. Jack's parents' desire to be missionaries explains why the story is set in Africa. However, this reason does not affect the plot of the story, so choice C is incorrect.

9. B: TEKS Standard (5.6)(E)

Both the lily and Jack were happy to receive something. In "Little White Lily," the lily was waiting for sunshine and rain. When the lily received them, she said it was "good," and they made the lily "happy again." In "Jack's First Christmas in Africa," Jack was happy to receive a surprise from his classmates, who recreated some of his American Christmas traditions. While Jack realized the value of friendship with his classmates, the lily does not experience friendship, so choice A is incorrect. While the lily was waiting for sunshine as "clothing and food," "Jack's First Christmas in Africa" does not state that Jack was looking forward to a meal. In fact, Jack was dreading the days leading up to Christmas because food like his mom's special Christmas cookies wouldn't be part of the holiday, so choice C is incorrect. While Jack receives care from his classmates, the lily does not receive care from another character. Additionally, Jack was not hoping that his classmates would do something to care for him, so choice D is incorrect.

10. A: TEKS Standard (5.6)(E)

In "Little White Lily," the lily is described as waiting "till the sun shone" and "waiting for the wet rain." Jack's Christmas celebration with his African classmates was a surprise, so it was not something he was waiting for. Both Jack and the lily were happy about what they received, so choice B is incorrect. The poem does not say that the lily was happy being by herself. The story also does not say that Jack wanted to make friends. In fact, "Jack's First Christmas in Africa" says that Jack had made friends, so choice C is incorrect. Jack was the one living in an unfamiliar place, not the lily, so choice D is incorrect.

11. C: TEKS Standard (5.6)(E)

Jack experiences the kindness of others when his classmates surprise him. However, the lily receives what she needs from nature, not from others being kind. Both Jack and the lily were happy to receive something, so choice A is incorrect. In the poem, the lily was "drooping" when waiting for the sunshine and rain, and in the story, Jack was sad to miss out on his Christmas traditions. Both characters were sad that they were missing something, so choice B is incorrect. Neither Jack nor the lily overcame a challenge through hard work, so choice D is incorrect.

12. C, E: TEKS Standard (5.6)(F)

Paragraph 5 says that pet hair from furry pets can be composted. While the paragraph does not name specific types of pets, the reader can conclude that, since dogs and cats are furry pets, their hair can break down into compost. Paragraph 5 does state that some types of cloth and wood can go in a compost pile and that adding these is an "unexpected" way to compost. Choices C and E are correct. Paragraph 5 says that only some types of cloth can go into a compost pile, so the reader cannot conclude that old clothing can always go into a compost pile. Choice A is incorrect. Paragraph 5 discusses surprising things that can be added to a compost pile in addition to scraps from plants, so choice B is incorrect. Paragraph 5 does not discuss the balance of wet and dry items in a compost pile, so the reader cannot make a conclusion about that information. Choice D is incorrect.

13. A: TEKS Standard (5.10)(A)

The author most likely wrote the passage to persuade the reader to try composting for themselves. The author provides details about composting that may encourage the reader to try it, such as that it is easy to start and can benefit the environment in many ways. While there is some information in the passage about how composting works, the main purpose of the passage is to persuade the reader. It is not meant to inform them about the science behind composting, so choice B is incorrect. While the passage has a persuasive purpose, the author is only speaking about composting. The author is not comparing composting to other actions that could reduce trash, so choice C is incorrect. The information about composting indoors is a small detail that supports the central claim of the passage, so choice D is incorrect.

14. A: TEKS Standard (5.6)(G)

Paragraph 3 states that a large container or area in the yard can be used for composting and that some people use worms to compost inside. This statement shows that choice A is correct. The idea that some items we throw away cannot go into a compost pile is supported by paragraph 6, not paragraph 3, so choice B is incorrect. Paragraph 3 describes ways to start composting that do not require a large container, so choice C is incorrect. The benefits to the environment are described in paragraphs 7 through 9, not in paragraph 3. This makes choice D incorrect.

15. D: TEKS Standard (5.9)(Eii)

The author supports the passage's central claim that composting can reduce trash by estimating that families throw away thousands of pounds of trash each year. The author also states that some of those materials could have been composted. The passage does not provide a chronological observation of a compost pile's progress, so choice A is incorrect. The author gives information about trash in landfills and explains how composting can reduce trash. However, the passage does not explain that the amount of trash that goes to landfills has increased over time, so choice B is incorrect. The passage is not written from a first-person perspective, and it does not describe the author's own experience, so choice C is incorrect.

16. D: TEKS Standard (5.6)(H)

Based on the information in the passage, the reader can conclude that composting does not need to cost a lot of money. The passage points out that composting can be done in a small bucket or other container outside. Many people already own these items. The passage also points out that compost is made of materials we would normally throw away, which also do not cost anything to use. These facts show that choice D is correct. While the passage points out that worms can be used in compost piles, there is no evidence to conclude that compost made from worms has the most nutrients, so choice A is incorrect. While the passage says that compost can provide nutrient-rich soil for plants, it does not compare it to fertilizer, so choice B is incorrect. The passage points out that composting helps save water. However, it does not state how much water it can save each family, so choice C is incorrect.

17. B: TEKS Standard (5.9)(Ei)

The passage explains how to create a compost pile and emphasizes that composting is easy. It also explains that composting helps the environment by supporting strong plants, saving water, and reducing trash. The passage does not describe the ideal amount of sunlight that a compost pile needs each day, so choice A is incorrect. The passage mentions a balance of wet and dry items and states that a pile should contain more dry items than wet items. It does not claim that a compost pile should have mostly wet items, so choice C is incorrect. While the passage says that composting can be done outside or with worms inside, it does not state that composting outside is easier, so choice D is incorrect.

18. B: TEKS Standard (5.9)(Eiii)

The passage describes composting and presents it as something that can benefit the environment. The groups that are most likely to be interested in this topic include people who care about the environment, so choice B is correct. Although the passage mentions that composting can create nutrient-rich soil that helps plants grow strong and healthy, the passage does not explain how plants grow, so choice A is incorrect. While composting can be considered a form of recycling, this passage does not give readers clear guidance on where to take their recycling, so choice C is incorrect. Compost creates usable rich soil that can be used for gardening. This means that people who do not like to garden are not likely to be interested in this passage, so choice D is incorrect.

19. A: TEKS Standard (5.9)(Diii)

The passage uses a chronological pattern and tells the events that led to George Lucas's success as a filmmaker, so choice A is correct. The passage does not contain specific information that compares and contrasts the main characters in George Lucas' various movies, so choice B is incorrect. The passage does not describe George Lucas's process for creating new movie characters, so choice C is incorrect. The information in the passage lists George Lucas' movies after *Star Wars* in the order they were made. It does not list them in order of most successful to least successful, so choice D is incorrect.

20. C: TEKS Standard (5.6)(G)

Paragraphs 3 and 4 support the idea that the success of George Lucas' first few movies was surprising. Paragraph 3 says that "the movie studio was concerned that people would not be interested" in his film *American Graffiti*. Paragraph 4 says that "the studio executives were worried that audiences would not like George's space adventure." Despite this, each film became a hit. George Lucas's first interest in film is explained in paragraph 2. Paragraphs 3 and 4 do not mention any of George Lucas's childhood goals, so choice A is incorrect. Paragraphs 3 and 4 do not describe George Lucas's opinion of his films. They suggest that he was more interested in science fiction than realistic fiction. However, this does not support the idea that he did not like *American Graffiti*, so choice B is incorrect. Paragraph 3 explains that George Lucas "rose to the challenge" to make a lighthearted comedy instead of a serious film. This shows that George Lucas accepted the challenge and tried something new. The passage does not show that he did not like to be challenged on his ideas, so choice D is incorrect.

21. B: TEKS Standard (5.7)(C)

This sentence clearly shows the success of George Lucas' first *Star Wars* movie by explaining that the movie made more money than any movie before it. The movie would not have made so much money if it had not attracted a large audience, so choice B is correct. Choice A shows that the studio executives thought George Lucas' movie would not be successful. This does not show the result of the movie's release, so choice A is incorrect. Choice C shows that the *Star Wars* series had many interested fans. However, it does not mention the success of George Lucas' first *Star Wars* movie, so it is incorrect. Choice D explains what George Lucas did after taking a break from making movies. This sentence does not show how successful the first *Star Wars* movie was, so choice D is incorrect.

22. A: TEKS Standard (5.3)(B)

The word *lighthearted* describes something that is fun and entertaining. Paragraph 3 supports this by describing *American Graffiti* as a "lighthearted comedy" with characters that are "funny" and "likable." The word *lighthearted* is also used in contrast to George Lucas' first film, which was "too serious." Even though *lighthearted* has the word *light* in it, the passage does not mention weight or describe floating, so choice B is incorrect. The word *lighthearted* is used to describe the mood of two of George Lucas' movies, not colors, so choice C is incorrect. Nothing in paragraphs 3 and 4 is described as fragile, weak, or anything similar, so choice D is incorrect.

23. D: TEKS Standard (5.7)(D)

Choice D includes key ideas from the beginning, middle, and end of the passage. This summary does not include unnecessary details, and it reflects the main idea of the passage. Choice A does not mention the movies that led George Lucas to make *Star Wars.* This information is a key idea in the passage, so choice A is incorrect. Choice B is incorrect because it does not mention the success of

American Graffiti or *Star Wars*. The success of George Lucas's movies is a key idea in the passage, so it should be included in the summary. Choice C is also missing these key ideas. Additionally, this summary is inaccurate because the passage states that George Lucas made the first *Star Wars* movie before he created the *Indiana Jones* movie character. Choice C is incorrect.

24. TEKS Standard (5.9)(Di)

George Lucas's story shows what can happen if you follow creative dreams and work hard. The passage explains that George Lucas did not give up on his creative ideas for movies, such as the *Star Wars* series. Paragraphs 3 and 5 show that George Lucas did not give up on his ideas. Paragraph 5 shows that making the films "was a lot of hard work," but paragraph 4 shows that *Star Wars* "made more money than any movie before it."

25. B: TEKS Standard (5.10)(A)

The author names a variety of characters in the *Star Wars* movie series in paragraph 1. With this list, the author explains that although the readers may not know of George Lucas, they have probably heard of some of his well-known heroes and villains. Choice B is correct. The author does not argue or attempt to persuade the reader that *Star Wars* is one of the best movies of all time, so choice A is incorrect. Paragraph 1 does not describe the chronological order in which George Lucas created the characters in *Star Wars*, so choice C is incorrect. Paragraph 1 only names some of George Lucas' most well-known movie characters. It does not reveal what inspired him to create these characters, so choice D is incorrect.

Extended Response

26. TEKS Standard (5.12)(B)

Please use the rubric below to make sure your response meets these criteria. Try to have a friend or family member grade your response for you or take a break after writing your response and return to grade it yourself with fresh eyes.

Below is an excerpt of the STAAR Grades 3-5 Informational Writing Rubric.

Score Point	Organization and Development of Ideas
3	• **Central idea is clear and fully developed** The central idea is clearly identifiable. The focus is consistent throughout, creating a response that is unified and easy to follow. • **Organization is effective** A purposeful structure that includes an effective introduction and conclusion is evident. The organizational structure is appropriate and effectively supports the development of the central idea. The sentences, paragraphs, or ideas are logically connected in purposeful and highly effective ways. • **Evidence is specific, well chosen, and relevant** The response includes relevant text-based evidence that is clearly explained and consistently supports and develops the central idea. For pairs in grades 3-5, evidence is drawn from at least one text. The response reflects a thorough understanding of the writing purpose. • **Expression of ideas is clear and effective** The writer's word choice is specific, purposeful, and enhances the response. Almost all sentences and phrases are effectively crafted to convey the writer's ideas and contribute to the overall quality of the response and the clarity of the message.

Score Point	Conventions
2	Student writing demonstrates **consistent command** of grade-level-appropriate conventions, including correct: • sentence construction • punctuation • capitalization • grammar • spelling The response has few errors, but those errors do not impact the clarity of the writing.

Revising

27. C: TEKS Standard (5.11)(Bii)

Sentence 4 explains when and where J.K. Rowling was born. Sentence 5 states that she was not able to get her stories published. A sentence added after sentence 4 should connect these ideas. Since sentence 5 is about Rowling trying to get her stories published, the new sentence should mention her writing. Choice C is the best choice because it shows that Rowling was dreaming of becoming a writer. This connects sentences 4 and 5 by showing what happened after she grew up and why she wanted to get her stories published. Choice A is incorrect because it gives unnecessary information. Choice B is incorrect because it does not connect the ideas in sentences 4 and 5. Choice D is incorrect because it gives information in the incorrect order. Rowling wrote *Harry Potter* after the event in sentence 6, so the sentence in choice D would come after sentence 6.

28. TEKS Standard (5.11)(C)

Sentence 14 is not clear because it gives information in an order that is hard to understand. It states that Harry continued to do things, and it states that readers wanted to know something. Readers wanted to find out what Harry did next. A revised version of sentence 14 should be similar to the following sentence: They could not wait to find out what Harry did next. The sentence should be complete, clear, and grammatically correct.

29. C: TEKS Standard (5.11)(Bi)

The transition at the beginning of sentence 18 is vague, or unclear. A more specific transition would help the reader understand how much time it took for Rowling to complete the *Harry Potter* series. Choice C is correct because it gives a specific amount of time. Choices A and D are incorrect because they are also unclear. They have the same meaning as *later*, which means that they do not give the reader any more information. While choice B is more specific than *later* and shows that a long amount of time passed, it is not as specific as choice C.

30. A: TEKS Standard (5.11)(C)

Sentence 21 says that two movies were made based on *Harry Potter and the Deathly Hallows*. This is the name of the last book in the *Harry Potter* series. Sentences 19 and 22 show that the movies were based on the books in the *Harry Potter* series. This shows that choice A is correct, since the last two movies in the film series were based on the last book. Choice B is incorrect because the movies were not based on the others in the film series. Choice C is incorrect because, while the passage says that the movies won awards, it does not support the idea that they were based on awards. Choice D is incorrect because there is only one author mentioned in this passage. The word *one* in sentence 21 cannot be replaced with *author* because there would need to be more than one author in order for there to be a last author.

31. D: TEKS Standard (5.11)(Bii)

Sentence 5 should be removed because it gives distracting and unnecessary information. Paragraph 1 introduces the topic and describes the appearance of walruses. Each sentence in the paragraph should support this topic and help create a transition into the next paragraph. Choice D is correct because the information in sentence 5 is unnecessary. The information in sentence 5 repeats information from sentence 3 and does not support sentence 4. It also does not create an effective transition to the next paragraph. Choice A is incorrect because sentence 1 prepares the reader for the rest of the information in the paragraph. Choice B is incorrect because sentence 2 introduces the topic of the passage and supports sentence 1. Choice C is incorrect because sentence 3 gives the reader the needed information and supports sentence 2.

32. B: TEKS Standard (5.11)(Bi)

Choice B is correct because it creates a clear transition from paragraph 1 to paragraph 2. It mentions that walruses look funny and adds that they are also very big. This helps the reader see the connection between the two paragraphs and shows what paragraph 2 is about. Choices A and B are incorrect because they are not related to the topic of the second paragraph. Choice D is incorrect because it is related to paragraph 3, not paragraph 2.

33. A: TEKS Standard (5.11)(Bi)

The transition word *before* is not clear and does not help the reader understand when walruses have brown skin. Choice A is correct because it is specific and helps the reader understand when walruses begin to change color. Choices B and C are incorrect because they are unclear. They do not provide enough information to help the reader understand the meaning of sentence 13. Choice D is more specific than choices B and C, but it still does not help the reader understand when in a walrus's life its coloring will change.

34. TEKS Standard (5.11)(C)

The new sentence should include the information given in both sentence 22 and sentence 23. Sentence 22 says that an adult walrus is able to fight back if it is attacked. Sentence 23 says that killer whales and polar bears try to stay away from walruses. This suggests that these predators avoid walruses because walruses can fight back. The new sentence should show this relationship. It should be similar to the following sentence: An adult walrus can fight back hard, so killer whales and polar bears prefer to avoid them if they can. The sentence may also be similar to the following: Because an adult walrus can fight back hard, killer whales and polar bears prefer to avoid them if they can. The sentence should be complete, clear, and free of any grammatical errors.

Editing

35. B: TEKS Standard (5.11)(Di)

Were is a plural verb that is used to describe the action done by a plural noun or pronoun. Since *She* is a singular pronoun, a singular verb should be used. *Were* should be changed to *was*, which is a singular noun. Choice B is correct. *She* is a subjective pronoun, and *her* is an objective pronoun. The word *she* is currently the subject of sentence 3. Since the subject should be a noun or subjective pronoun, *she* is used correctly, and choice B is incorrect. There is no need to add a comma after *puppy*, since commas are not always added before prepositional phrases, so choice C is incorrect. The word *time* is spelled using a silent *-e*. The word is spelled correctly in sentence 3, so choice D is incorrect.

36. C: TEKS Standard (5.2)(Biii)

The word *barking* is spelled incorrectly in sentence 7. *Barking* is spelled using the verb *bark* and the suffix *-ing*. Since this word uses the suffix *-ing*, it is not spelled *barkeeng*, so choice C is correct. *Know* is a present tense verb, and *knew* is a past tense verb. However, the words *did not* are used before *know* in sentence 7. Since the word *did* is a past tense verb, it makes the phrase *did not know* function as a past tense verb. *Know* does not need to be changed to *knew*, so choice A is incorrect. The word *dog* is the second item in a list of three items. It comes before *and*, so it should be followed by a comma. Choice B is incorrect. Choice D is incorrect because *barkeeng* should be changed to *barking*.

37. B: TEKS Standard (5.2)(Bvi)

The word *creeping* is spelled using the verb *creep* and the suffix *-ing*. Sometimes, when adding a suffix to a word that ends in a consonant, the consonant must be doubled. Usually, the consonant is doubled when the suffix begins with a vowel and the root word ends with a single vowel followed by a single consonant. In this case, *creep* is spelled using two vowels before the last consonant. This means that the consonant *p* does not need to be doubled when the suffix *-ing* is added to *creep*. Choice B is correct, since *creepping* is misspelled. *Came* is a is a past tense verb, and *come* is a present tense verb. Sentence 10 is in the past tense, so it should be written using past tense verbs. *Came* is used correctly in sentence 10, so choice A is incorrect. Choices C and D suggest changing words in ways that would change the meaning of the sentence. The sentence makes sense, and the words *slowly* and *at* are used correctly, so choices C and D are incorrect.

38. B: TEKS Standard (5.11)(Dxi)

Histery is a misspelling for the word *history*, so choice B is correct. The word *figures* is used before a prepositional phrase. While commas are often used after prepositional phrases, they are not needed before them, so choice A is incorrect. The first independent clause says there are many remarkable athletes in history. The second independent clause says that Roger Staubach is better than they are. The best coordinating conjunction to use between these sentences is one that shows contrast. *But* is the correct conjunction to use in sentence 1, so choice C is incorrect. The Dallas Cowboys are a football team, and their team's name is a proper noun. All the nouns in a proper noun should be capitalized, so choice D is incorrect.

39. After: TEKS Standard (5.11)(Dviii)

This sentence describes what Roger Staubach did following his time in high school, so *after* is the best word to use at the beginning of this sentence. Using *when* or *as* would suggest that he went to high school and was in the Navy at the same time. This is not what the sentence should say, so those choices are incorrect. *Until* suggests that he joined the Navy before he was in high school. This is also not what the sentence should say, so it is an incorrect choice.

40. D: TEKS Standard (5.11)(Diii)

The word *team* is a collective noun. This means that it is a singular noun that represents multiple members. So, even though there are multiple players on a team, the word *team* is singular, so it does not need to include an *s* at the end. Choice D is correct. *Through* would not make sense as the first word in sentence 5, so choice A is incorrect. The word *Academy* is the last word in a prepositional phrase. When a long prepositional phrase starts a sentence, it should be followed by a comma, so choice B is incorrect. *Led* is a past tense verb, and *leads* is a present tense verb. Sentence 5 is in the past tense, so *led* is used correctly, and choice C is incorrect.

41. D: TEKS Standard (5.11)(D)

This sentence does not contain any spelling or grammar errors, so choice D is correct. *He* is a subjective pronoun, and *him* is an objective pronoun. The word *he* is used as the subject of sentence 9, so it is used correctly, and choice A is incorrect. When used in a statement, *couldn't* is a contraction for the past tense verb phrase *could not*. *Can't* is a contraction for *cannot*, which is used in present tense sentences. Sentence 9 is in the past tense, so *couldn't* is used correctly, and choice B is incorrect. In the word *professionally*, the *ss* is pronounced like *sh*, though it is spelled *ss*. *Professionally* is spelled correctly, so choice C is incorrect.

Practice Test #3

To take this additional STAAR practice test, visit our online resources page:
mometrix.com/resources719/staarg5rla

How to Overcome Test Anxiety

Just the thought of taking a test is enough to make most people a little nervous. A test is an important event that can have a long-term impact on your future, so it's important to take it seriously and it's natural to feel anxious about performing well. But just because anxiety is normal, that doesn't mean that it's helpful in test taking, or that you should simply accept it as part of your life. Anxiety can have a variety of effects. These effects can be mild, like making you feel slightly nervous, or severe, like blocking your ability to focus or remember even a simple detail.

If you experience test anxiety—whether severe or mild—it's important to know how to beat it. To discover this, first you need to understand what causes test anxiety.

Causes of Test Anxiety

While we often think of anxiety as an uncontrollable emotional state, it can actually be caused by simple, practical things. One of the most common causes of test anxiety is that a person does not feel adequately prepared for their test. This feeling can be the result of many different issues such as poor study habits or lack of organization, but the most common culprit is time management. Starting to study too late, failing to organize your study time to cover all of the material, or being distracted while you study will mean that you're not well prepared for the test. This may lead to cramming the night before, which will cause you to be physically and mentally exhausted for the test. Poor time management also contributes to feelings of stress, fear, and hopelessness as you realize you are not well prepared but don't know what to do about it.

Other times, test anxiety is not related to your preparation for the test but comes from unresolved fear. This may be a past failure on a test, or poor performance on tests in general. It may come from comparing yourself to others who seem to be performing better or from the stress of living up to expectations. Anxiety may be driven by fears of the future—how failure on this test would affect your educational and career goals. These fears are often completely irrational, but they can still negatively impact your test performance.

Elements of Test Anxiety

As mentioned earlier, test anxiety is considered to be an emotional state, but it has physical and mental components as well. Sometimes you may not even realize that you are suffering from test anxiety until you notice the physical symptoms. These can include trembling hands, rapid heartbeat, sweating, nausea, and tense muscles. Extreme anxiety may lead to fainting or vomiting. Obviously, any of these symptoms can have a negative impact on testing. It is important to recognize them as soon as they begin to occur so that you can address the problem before it damages your performance.

The mental components of test anxiety include trouble focusing and inability to remember learned information. During a test, your mind is on high alert, which can help you recall information and stay focused for an extended period of time. However, anxiety interferes with your mind's natural processes, causing you to blank out, even on the questions you know well. The strain of testing during anxiety makes it difficult to stay focused, especially on a test that may take several hours. Extreme anxiety can take a huge mental toll, making it difficult not only to recall test information but even to understand the test questions or pull your thoughts together.

Effects of Test Anxiety

Test anxiety is like a disease—if left untreated, it will get progressively worse. Anxiety leads to poor performance, and this reinforces the feelings of fear and failure, which in turn lead to poor performances on subsequent tests. It can grow from a mild nervousness to a crippling condition. If allowed to progress, test anxiety can have a big impact on your schooling, and consequently on your future.

Test anxiety can spread to other parts of your life. Anxiety on tests can become anxiety in any stressful situation, and blanking on a test can turn into panicking in a job situation. But fortunately, you don't have to let anxiety rule your testing and determine your grades. There are a number of relatively simple steps you can take to move past anxiety and function normally on a test and in the rest of life.

Physical Steps for Beating Test Anxiety

While test anxiety is a serious problem, the good news is that it can be overcome. It doesn't have to control your ability to think and remember information. While it may take time, you can begin taking steps today to beat anxiety.

Just as your first hint that you may be struggling with anxiety comes from the physical symptoms, the first step to treating it is also physical. Rest is crucial for having a clear, strong mind. If you are tired, it is much easier to give in to anxiety. But if you establish good sleep habits, your body and mind will be ready to perform optimally, without the strain of exhaustion. Additionally, sleeping well helps you to retain information better, so you're more likely to recall the answers when you see the test questions.

Getting good sleep means more than going to bed on time. It's important to allow your brain time to relax. Take study breaks from time to time so it doesn't get overworked, and don't study right before bed. Take time to rest your mind before trying to rest your body, or you may find it difficult to fall asleep.

Along with sleep, other aspects of physical health are important in preparing for a test. Good nutrition is vital for good brain function. Sugary foods and drinks may give a burst of energy but this burst is followed by a crash, both physically and emotionally. Instead, fuel your body with protein and vitamin-rich foods.

Also, drink plenty of water. Dehydration can lead to headaches and exhaustion, especially if your brain is already under stress from the rigors of the test. Particularly if your test is a long one, drink water during the breaks. And if possible, take an energy-boosting snack to eat between sections.

Along with sleep and diet, a third important part of physical health is exercise. Maintaining a steady workout schedule is helpful, but even taking 5-minute study breaks to walk can help get your blood pumping faster and clear your head. Exercise also releases endorphins, which contribute to a positive feeling and can help combat test anxiety.

When you nurture your physical health, you are also contributing to your mental health. If your body is healthy, your mind is much more likely to be healthy as well. So take time to rest, nourish your body with healthy food and water, and get moving as much as possible. Taking these physical steps will make you stronger and more able to take the mental steps necessary to overcome test anxiety.

Mental Steps for Beating Test Anxiety

Working on the mental side of test anxiety can be more challenging, but as with the physical side, there are clear steps you can take to overcome it. As mentioned earlier, test anxiety often stems from lack of preparation, so the obvious solution is to prepare for the test. Effective studying may be the most important weapon you have for beating test anxiety, but you can and should employ several other mental tools to combat fear.

First, boost your confidence by reminding yourself of past success—tests or projects that you aced. If you're putting as much effort into preparing for this test as you did for those, there's no reason you should expect to fail here. Work hard to prepare; then trust your preparation.

Second, surround yourself with encouraging people. It can be helpful to find a study group, but be sure that the people you're around will encourage a positive attitude. If you spend time with others who are anxious or cynical, this will only contribute to your own anxiety. Look for others who are motivated to study hard from a desire to succeed, not from a fear of failure.

Third, reward yourself. A test is physically and mentally tiring, even without anxiety, and it can be helpful to have something to look forward to. Plan an activity following the test, regardless of the outcome, such as going to a movie or getting ice cream.

When you are taking the test, if you find yourself beginning to feel anxious, remind yourself that you know the material. Visualize successfully completing the test. Then take a few deep, relaxing breaths and return to it. Work through the questions carefully but with confidence, knowing that you are capable of succeeding.

Developing a healthy mental approach to test taking will also aid in other areas of life. Test anxiety affects more than just the actual test—it can be damaging to your mental health and even contribute to depression. It's important to beat test anxiety before it becomes a problem for more than testing.

Study Strategy

Being prepared for the test is necessary to combat anxiety, but what does being prepared look like? You may study for hours on end and still not feel prepared. What you need is a strategy for test prep. The next few pages outline our recommended steps to help you plan out and conquer the challenge of preparation.

Step 1: Scope Out the Test

Learn everything you can about the format (multiple choice, essay, etc.) and what will be on the test. Gather any study materials, course outlines, or sample exams that may be available. Not only will this help you to prepare, but knowing what to expect can help to alleviate test anxiety.

Step 2: Map Out the Material

Look through the textbook or study guide and make note of how many chapters or sections it has. Then divide these over the time you have. For example, if a book has 15 chapters and you have five days to study, you need to cover three chapters each day. Even better, if you have the time, leave an extra day at the end for overall review after you have gone through the material in depth.

If time is limited, you may need to prioritize the material. Look through it and make note of which sections you think you already have a good grasp on, and which need review. While you are studying, skim quickly through the familiar sections and take more time on the challenging parts.

Write out your plan so you don't get lost as you go. Having a written plan also helps you feel more in control of the study, so anxiety is less likely to arise from feeling overwhelmed at the amount to cover.

Step 3: Gather Your Tools

Decide what study method works best for you. Do you prefer to highlight in the book as you study and then go back over the highlighted portions? Or do you type out notes of the important information? Or is it helpful to make flashcards that you can carry with you? Assemble the pens, index cards, highlighters, post-it notes, and any other materials you may need so you won't be distracted by getting up to find things while you study.

If you're having a hard time retaining the information or organizing your notes, experiment with different methods. For example, try color-coding by subject with colored pens, highlighters, or post-it notes. If you learn better by hearing, try recording yourself reading your notes so you can listen while in the car, working out, or simply sitting at your desk. Ask a friend to quiz you from your flashcards, or try teaching someone the material to solidify it in your mind.

Step 4: Create Your Environment

It's important to avoid distractions while you study. This includes both the obvious distractions like visitors and the subtle distractions like an uncomfortable chair (or a too-comfortable couch that makes you want to fall asleep). Set up the best study environment possible: good lighting and a comfortable work area. If background music helps you focus, you may want to turn it on, but otherwise keep the room quiet. If you are using a computer to take notes, be sure you don't have any other windows open, especially applications like social media, games, or anything else that could distract you. Silence your phone and turn off notifications. Be sure to keep water close by so you stay hydrated while you study (but avoid unhealthy drinks and snacks).

Also, take into account the best time of day to study. Are you freshest first thing in the morning? Try to set aside some time then to work through the material. Is your mind clearer in the afternoon or evening? Schedule your study session then. Another method is to study at the same time of day that you will take the test, so that your brain gets used to working on the material at that time and will be ready to focus at test time.

Step 5: Study!

Once you have done all the study preparation, it's time to settle into the actual studying. Sit down, take a few moments to settle your mind so you can focus, and begin to follow your study plan. Don't give in to distractions or let yourself procrastinate. This is your time to prepare so you'll be ready to fearlessly approach the test. Make the most of the time and stay focused.

Of course, you don't want to burn out. If you study too long you may find that you're not retaining the information very well. Take regular study breaks. For example, taking five minutes out of every hour to walk briskly, breathing deeply and swinging your arms, can help your mind stay fresh.

As you get to the end of each chapter or section, it's a good idea to do a quick review. Remind yourself of what you learned and work on any difficult parts. When you feel that you've mastered the material, move on to the next part. At the end of your study session, briefly skim through your notes again.

But while review is helpful, cramming last minute is NOT. If at all possible, work ahead so that you won't need to fit all your study into the last day. Cramming overloads your brain with more information than it can process and retain, and your tired mind may struggle to recall even previously learned information when it is overwhelmed with last-minute study. Also, the urgent nature of cramming and the stress placed on your brain contribute to anxiety. You'll be more likely to go to the test feeling unprepared and having trouble thinking clearly.

So don't cram, and don't stay up late before the test, even just to review your notes at a leisurely pace. Your brain needs rest more than it needs to go over the information again. In fact, plan to finish your studies by noon or early afternoon the day before the test. Give your brain the rest of the day to relax or focus on other things, and get a good night's sleep. Then you will be fresh for the test and better able to recall what you've studied.

Step 6: Take a Practice Test

Many courses offer sample tests, either online or in the study materials. This is an excellent resource to check whether you have mastered the material, as well as to prepare for the test format and environment.

Check the test format ahead of time: the number of questions, the type (multiple choice, free response, etc.), and the time limit. Then create a plan for working through them. For example, if you have 30 minutes to take a 60-question test, your limit is 30 seconds per question. Spend less time on the questions you know well so that you can take more time on the difficult ones.

If you have time to take several practice tests, take the first one open book, with no time limit. Work through the questions at your own pace and make sure you fully understand them. Gradually work up to taking a test under test conditions: sit at a desk with all study materials put away and set a timer. Pace yourself to make sure you finish the test with time to spare and go back to check your answers if you have time.

After each test, check your answers. On the questions you missed, be sure you understand why you missed them. Did you misread the question (tests can use tricky wording)? Did you forget the information? Or was it something you hadn't learned? Go back and study any shaky areas that the practice tests reveal.

Taking these tests not only helps with your grade, but also aids in combating test anxiety. If you're already used to the test conditions, you're less likely to worry about it, and working through tests until you're scoring well gives you a confidence boost. Go through the practice tests until you feel comfortable, and then you can go into the test knowing that you're ready for it.

Test Tips

On test day, you should be confident, knowing that you've prepared well and are ready to answer the questions. But aside from preparation, there are several test day strategies you can employ to maximize your performance.

First, as stated before, get a good night's sleep the night before the test (and for several nights before that, if possible). Go into the test with a fresh, alert mind rather than staying up late to study.

Try not to change too much about your normal routine on the day of the test. It's important to eat a nutritious breakfast, but if you normally don't eat breakfast at all, consider eating just a protein bar. If you're a coffee drinker, go ahead and have your normal coffee. Just make sure you time it so that the caffeine doesn't wear off right in the middle of your test. Avoid sugary beverages, and drink enough water to stay hydrated but not so much that you need a restroom break 10 minutes into the test. If your test isn't first thing in the morning, consider going for a walk or doing a light workout before the test to get your blood flowing.

Allow yourself enough time to get ready, and leave for the test with plenty of time to spare so you won't have the anxiety of scrambling to arrive in time. Another reason to be early is to select a good seat. It's helpful to sit away from doors and windows, which can be distracting. Find a good seat, get out your supplies, and settle your mind before the test begins.

When the test begins, start by going over the instructions carefully, even if you already know what to expect. Make sure you avoid any careless mistakes by following the directions.

Then begin working through the questions, pacing yourself as you've practiced. If you're not sure on an answer, don't spend too much time on it, and don't let it shake your confidence. Either skip it and come back later, or eliminate as many wrong answers as possible and guess among the remaining ones. Don't dwell on these questions as you continue—put them out of your mind and focus on what lies ahead.

Be sure to read all of the answer choices, even if you're sure the first one is the right answer. Sometimes you'll find a better one if you keep reading. But don't second-guess yourself if you do immediately know the answer. Your gut instinct is usually right. Don't let test anxiety rob you of the information you know.

If you have time at the end of the test (and if the test format allows), go back and review your answers. Be cautious about changing any, since your first instinct tends to be correct, but make sure you didn't misread any of the questions or accidentally mark the wrong answer choice. Look over any you skipped and make an educated guess.

At the end, leave the test feeling confident. You've done your best, so don't waste time worrying about your performance or wishing you could change anything. Instead, celebrate the successful completion of this test. And finally, use this test to learn how to deal with anxiety even better next time.

Review Video: Test Anxiety
Visit mometrix.com/academy and enter code: 100340

Important Qualification

Not all anxiety is created equal. If your test anxiety is causing major issues in your life beyond the classroom or testing center, or if you are experiencing troubling physical symptoms related to your anxiety, it may be a sign of a serious physiological or psychological condition. If this sounds like your situation, we strongly encourage you to seek professional help.

Online Resources

Due to our efforts to try to keep this book to a manageable length, we've created a link that will give you access to all of your online resources:

mometrix.com/resources719/staarg5rla

It's Your Moment, Let's Celebrate It!

Share your story @mometrixtestpreparation